CW00665266

20
20

Twenty Years of Amazing Things That Have Changed Our World

Sam Berry

2020

Text by Sarah Herman

An Hachette UK Company
www.hachette.co.uk

Summersdale Publishers Ltd
Part of Octopus Publishing Group Limited
Carmelite House
50 Victoria Embankment
LONDON
EC4Y 0DZ
UK

www.summersdale.com

Printed and bound in China

ISBN: 978-1-78783-039-4

Disclaimer: All facts are correct to the best of the author's knowledge at the time of going to press.

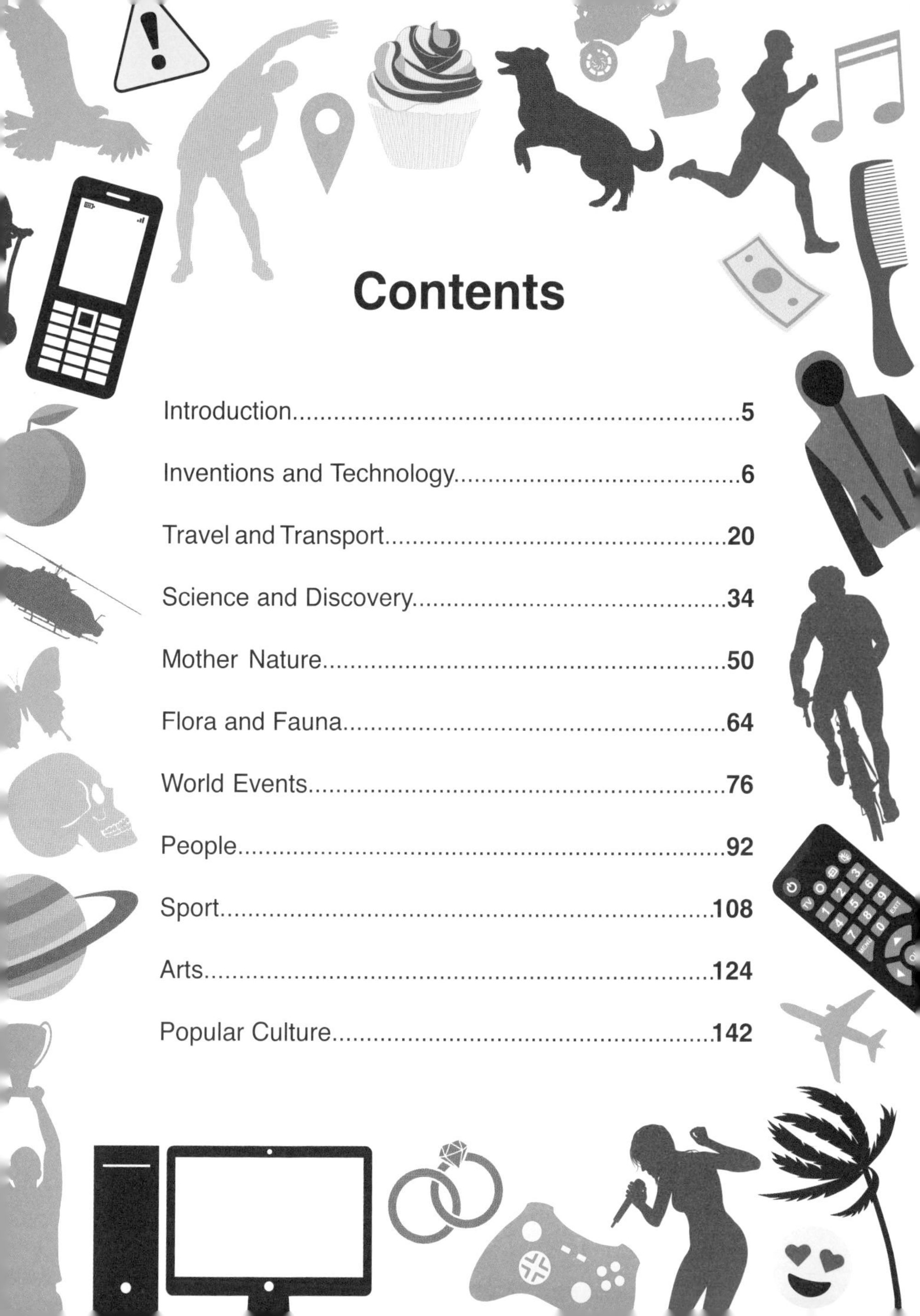

Contents

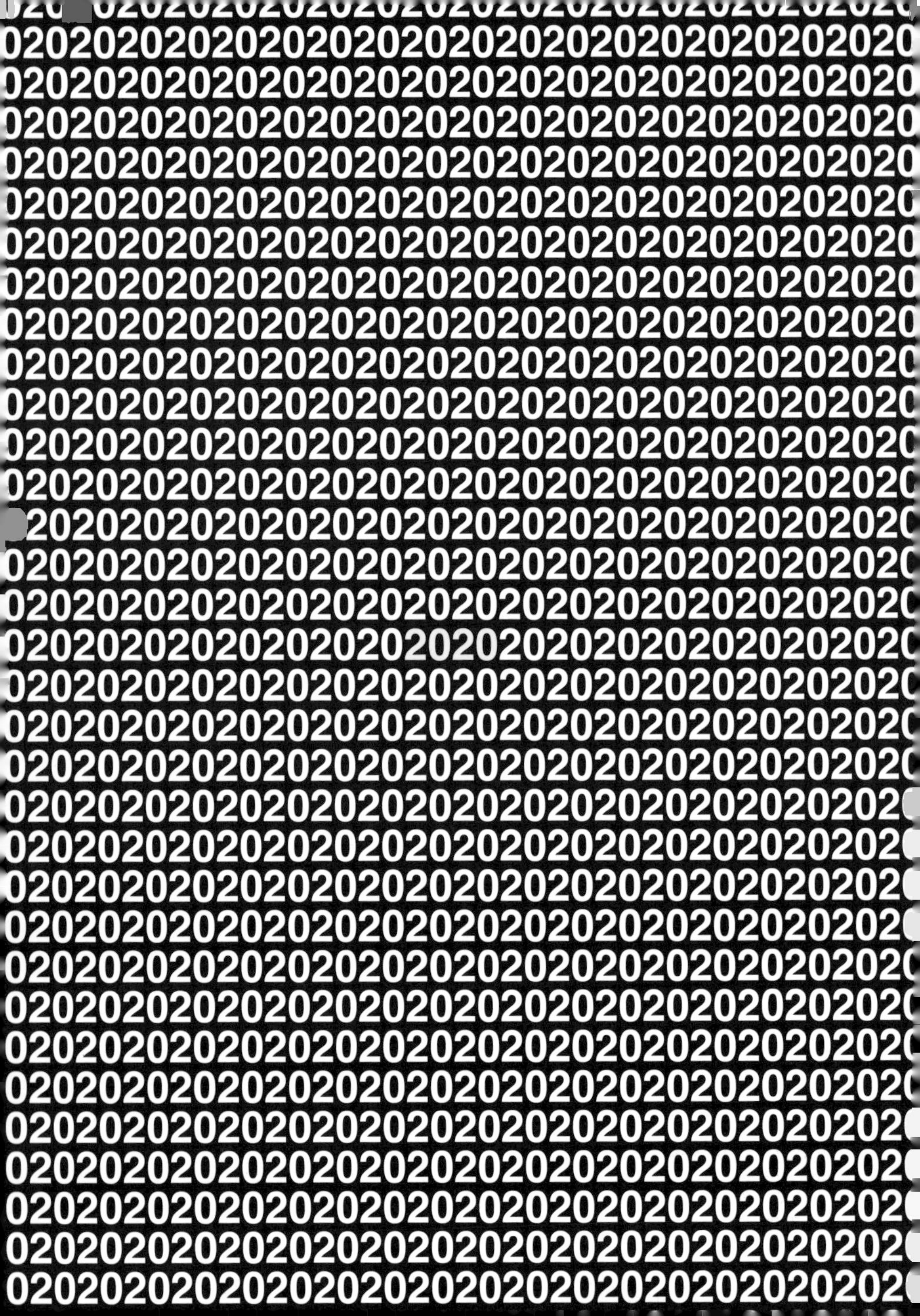

Introduction

It seems a lifetime ago when skies around the world lit up with fireworks to announce the start of a new millennium (and for younger readers, it really is). It was the end of the 'Y2K bug' panic and the birth of a new era of scientific discovery, space exploration and technological innovation. From phones to Furbies and viral videos to virtual reality, the world we live in has changed dramatically in the two decades that followed.

This book takes a look back at the last 20 years, listing the amazing cultural, political and geographical events that had an impact. Whether it's fashion trends or food fads, Nobel Prizes or famous artworks, volcanic eruptions or severe storms, these are the significant moments that have shaped the twenty-first century so far. It includes the biggest blunders by world leaders, the most exciting dinosaur discoveries, some seriously shocking sports scandals, and the reality shows that changed the face of TV forever.

What was so special about the World Athletics Championship in 2009? Do you know where to find the world's tallest building? Who faced 66 counts of crimes against humanity in 2002? And why was Michael Moore booed off stage when he won an Oscar? Find out all of this and more!

20 Technical Innovations

1. Unveiled in 1999, it wasn't until the year 2000 that manufacturers started to incorporate the now-ubiquitous Bluetooth technology into mobile phones and computers.

2. 2001 saw the release of Apple's portable music player, the iPod. Along with Apple's iTunes software, it transformed the way people accessed and listened to music.

3. That year also saw a self-powered AbioCor artificial heart replace a human heart for the first time.

4. Before 2003, and the introduction of free calling through telecommunications tool Skype, talking to people in other countries was very expensive and video chatting was virtually non-existent.

5. The ultimate social networking website – Facebook – was launched in 2004 and a world of poking, liking, sharing and posting began.

6. YouTube is the world's most popular video-sharing website. It's hard to believe it only started in 2005 – in June 2018 it counted over 5 billion views a day.

7. The Global Positioning System (GPS) was originally developed in the 1970s for military use, but it wasn't until 2005 that the first modernised GPS satellite was launched and became commercially available.

8. Increased physical engagement with video games emerged seemingly out of nowhere with the 2006 release of Nintendo's Wii console, offering titles such as *Wii Play* and *Wii Sports*.

9. No tech innovation list would be complete without the Apple iPhone, first launched in 2007. Following on from the 1992 IBM Simon and the 2004 Nokia 7710, it featured a finger-controlled touchscreen – and changed the face of mobiles forever.

10. In 2007, Google launched Street View in the United States, providing panoramic views of city streets as part of its maps service.

11. The Amazon Kindle eBook reader and its integrated eBook store came onto the market in 2007. Since then, it has become the go-to reader and service for digital book consumers.

12. The release of Google's Android mobile phone operating system in 2008 meant other mobile manufacturers could compete with the iPhone's success.

13. At a time when music piracy was rife, music-streaming platform Spotify launched its free and legal subscription service in 2008, changing the way millions of people access music around the world.

14. 4G data service standards were created in 2008, too, giving people higher data capacity and allowing mobile gaming, video conferencing and cloud computing to truly take off. The years 2019 and 2020 will see the introduction of 5G. With speeds of up to 100 gigabits per second, 5G is set to be as much as 1,000 times faster than 4G!

15. The year 2009 saw the release of the first commercially available 3D printer: the BfB RapMan 3D printer was available in kit form, opening up the world of 3D printing to the masses.

16. Cinema-goers could see the full potential of the latest 3D cinema technology with the 2009 release of James Cameron's *Avatar*. It was shot using the HD Reality Camera System, rather than on film.

17. Apple took another giant leap with the launch of the first iPad in 2010 – it was a tablet PC that captured the public's imagination and remains the most popular of its kind.

18. While electric cars currently make up a small portion of the overall automobile market, the top-selling highway-capable electric car at the time of writing is the Nissan Leaf, first sold in 2010.

19. The new millennium saw numerous major companies and research organisations developing prototypes of 'self-driving' cars, ranging from General Motors and Audi to Oxford University and Google. In 2013, four US states passed laws permitting 'autonomous cars' on public roads. The United Kingdom followed suit in 2015.

20. Amazon launched its Echo speaker in 2014 with virtual assistant Alexa – connecting your home to the internet. Google followed a year later with its Home Hub.

20 IMPRESSIVE ENGINEERING FEATS

1. In 2001, the environmentally aware Eden Project opened in Cornwall, UK. The tourist attraction harnesses unique architecture and technology to simulate two diverse ecological communities, known as biomes.

2. Completed in 2008, the Large Hadron Collider at Conseil Européen pour la Recherche Nucléaire (CERN) in Switzerland is one of the most advanced research facilities in the world. In 2012, it confirmed the existence of the Higgs boson particle.

3. NASA's three Mars rovers *Opportunity*, *Spirit* and *Curiosity* landed on Mars in 2004 and 2012. They were built to withstand the inhospitable Martian environment, and to study the planet's climate, geology and microscopic particles. *Opportunity* lasted 50 times longer than planned and was only declared dead in February 2019.

4. NASA also came up with the Sky Crane manoeuvre to land the heavier *Curiosity* rover safely on Mars. The landing gear consisted of an eight-rocket jetpack and parachute device attached to the rover and helped slow its descent.

5. The Yangtze River in Sandouping, China, was transformed when the Three Gorges Dam – 2,335 metres (7,660 feet) long – became fully operational in 2012. It's currently the world's largest power station, with a generating capacity of 22,500 MW.

6. Founded in 2002 by Tesla owner Elon Musk, in 2011 SpaceX successfully developed a reusable space launch system. In 2018, it sent a rocket to orbit the sun with Musk's Tesla car on board, and in 2019 it conducted the maiden flight of *Crew Dragon*, a spacecraft able to carry humans.

7. The year 2008 saw ground broken on the Brenner Base Tunnel project, a railway tunnel that connects northern and southern Europe and is 55 kilometres (34 miles) long. It reaches through the base of the Brenner massif part of the Alps.

8. The tallest bridge in human history to date was completed in 2004. The award-winning Millau Viaduct spans the River Tarn valley in southern France. Each post is 343 metres (1,125 feet) tall.

9. In 2007, Michael Pritchard unveiled his LifeSaver bottle – a water purification system ideal for humanitarians in disaster zones, the military, and those with no supply of clean drinking water.

10. In 2012, Singapore became home to one of the largest garden projects in the world. 'Gardens by the Bay' is a billion-dollar techno-garden theme park. The most recognisable attraction is the Supertree Grove, a collection of huge cyborg-looking trees.

11. The Leaning Tower of Pisa, Italy, was knocked off its perch in 2010 when Abu Dhabi's (UAE) Capital Gate was named the furthest man-made leaning building, with an impressive 18-degree tilt.

12. The Metropol Parasol in Seville, Spain, said to be the largest wooden structure in the world, was completed in 2011. It's home to a museum and a restaurant, as well as providing shelter for a marketplace.

13. The Venice Tide Barrier Project (MOSE), Italy – the world's largest flood prevention project – was started in 2003. It consists of 78 seabed gates that release water and float when the tide rises.

14. Dubai, UAE, started ambitious plans to construct three man-made Palm Islands in 2001. In 2007, the first residents moved into their new homes on Palm Jumeirah. This first island alone added over 60 kilometres (37 miles) of new coastline. The other two are awaiting construction.

15. At 326 metres (1,070 feet), the cliffside Bailong Elevator in China's Zhangjiajie National Forest Park is the highest and heaviest outdoor elevator in the world. It opened to the public in 2002.

16. With the aim of transforming 500,000 acres of desert into farmland with a unique irrigation system, the New Valley Project in Egypt's Western Desert got underway in 2005.

17. Completed in 2005, the curved Langkawi Sky Bridge is a pedestrian walkway at the top of Mount Mat Cincang, Malaysia. At 605 metres (2,000 feet) high, it's one of the highest bridges of this type in the world.

18. German car producer Volkswagen threw out the rule book for car factories when it opened *Die Gläserne Manufaktur* (The Transparent Factory) in the heart of Dresden, Germany, in 2001. The glass structure allowed buyers of the luxury model Phaeton to see their cars made at every step from start to finish, and then to drive it straight off the production line.

19. To date, the world's longest bridge is China's Danyang-Kunshan Grand Bridge, opened in 2011. It is 165 kilometres (102 miles) long and carries the Beijing–Shanghai High-Speed Railway.

20. China Central TV's headquarters in Beijing opened in 2012. Its extreme cantilever architecture won it a 2013 Structural Award from the Institution of Structural Engineers.

20 REALLY TALL STRUCTURES

1. Currently the world's tallest building, standing at 829.8 metres (2,722 feet) high, is Burj Khalifa in Dubai, UAE. It opened in 2010 and broke a number of other records, including having the most storeys, highest observation deck and tallest service elevator.

2. When it was completed in 2013, the 128-storey Shanghai Tower stood at 632 metres (2,073 feet) – impressive, but only tall enough to take second place.

3. For six years Taiwan was the proud home of the world's tallest building: Taipei 101 reached a height of 508 metres (1,667 feet). It was overtaken in 2010 by Dubai's Burj Khalifa.

4. At present, North America's tallest building, completed in 2013, is the One World Trade Center in New York. At 541.3 metres (1,776 feet), it is the main building of the new World Trade Center complex that was rebuilt after the events of 9/11.

5. As of 2014, New York is also home to the tallest residential skyscraper – 432 Park Avenue. For a building to be considered residential, 85 per cent of its total floor area has to be for this use. This record will be broken by the New York Steinway Tower reaching 435 metres (1,427 feet), once finished in 2019.

6. Russia is already home to Europe's tallest buildings. But once finished in 2019, the Lakhta Centre in St. Petersburg will reach 462 metres (1,516 feet) and add nearly 100 metres (328 feet) to the European record, so far held by the Federation Tower in Moscow.

7. Oceania's tallest building went up in 2005 and can be found on Australia's Gold Coast at Surfers Paradise, Queensland. At just 322.5 metres (1,058 feet), the Q1 doesn't even make the top 60 tallest buildings in the world.

8. Across the whole South American continent, the Torre Costanera in Santiago, Chile, is the tallest structure. Built in 2012, it is 300 metres (984 feet) tall and contains 64 storeys.

9. Surprisingly, Africa's tallest building is still the Carlton Centre in Johannesburg, South Africa, completed in 1973. It measures 201 metres (659 feet). In 2019, after a reign of 46 years, it will finally be overtaken by The Leonardo in Sandton, another South African skyscraper, which will be only 26 metres (85 feet) taller.

10. Burj Khalifa in Dubai, UAE, will lose its title as the world's tallest skyscraper when the Jeddah Tower in Jeddah, Saudi Arabia, reaches completion in 2021. It will be the first building to reach 1 kilometre (3,280 feet) in height.

11. London hosts 18 of the 20 tallest buildings in the United Kingdom. The aptly named Shard is the tallest, topping One Canada Square (in second place) by 70 metres (230 feet). Finished in 2012 and reaching a height of 306 metres (1,004 feet), it's become an iconic part of the London skyline.

12. In France, Paris is home to the country's tallest building – Tour First – which was completed in 2011. At 231 metres (758 feet), it's still dwarfed by the Eiffel Tower at 324 metres (1,063 feet).

13. The Eiffel Tower is around half the size of Japan's tallest structure, Tokyo Sky Tree, which was completed in 2011 and is the tallest self-supporting tower in the world.

14. For high-flying thrills, the 2005 Kingda Ka at Six Flags Great Adventure, New Jersey, USA, is the tallest roller coaster in the world. Passengers reach heights of a vomit-inducing 139 metres (456 feet).

15. It's slightly less exciting, but the Swissmill (Kornhaus) in Zurich, Switzerland, became the tallest operating grain elevator in the world in 2016. It was an existing silo, which was increased in height from only 38 metres (124 feet) to 118 metres (387 feet) and can now hold 28,450 tonnes (28,000 tons) of grain.

16. In Yalong, China, you'll find the tallest concrete arch dam. Harnessing hydropower on the Jinping Bend of the Yalong River, the Jinping-I Dam measures 305 metres (1,000 feet) in height and was completed in 2013.

17. From 2014, tourists could soak up the views from the High Roller in Las Vegas, Nevada, USA. It is the world's tallest Ferris wheel, at a staggering 167.7 metres (550 feet).

18. You'd need to be very energetic to make it to the top of the GE 3.4-137 wind turbine in Naturstromspeicher Gaildorf, Germany. It was built in 2017 and is the world's tallest wind turbine, measuring 246.5 metres (808 feet).

19. In 2018, India's Prime Minister Narendra Modi inaugurated the monumental Statue of Unity in Gujarat India's western-most state. Including the base, the statue of independence activist Sardar Vallabhbhai Patel measures 240 metres (787 feet) and is the tallest in the world.

20. Air Traffic Control at Kuala Lumpur International Airport, Malaysia, have the honour of doing their job from Tower West – in 2013, it was the tallest ATC tower in the world at 133.8 metres (440 feet) tall.

20 COOLEST ROBOTS

1. Keepon, an interactive toy to help researchers and doctors to study social development and coordination in children, went viral in 2007 when a video of the robot dancing was uploaded online.
2. After the 9/11 terrorist attacks, shoe-box-size PackBots robots, each fitted with four cameras, were used to search for victims and assess the structural integrity of the debris by sending back rough images from hard-to-reach places. The US military also deployed 2,000 of them in Afghanistan to search caves for insurgents.
3. In 2007, the creators of interactive toy Furby launched Pleo – an adorable dinosaur robot featuring a camera-based vision system, touch sensors, and 14 force feedback sensors.
4. Boston Dynamics, famous for its advanced humanoid and canine automatons, began sale of a four-legged SpotMini in 2019. The robot is able to inspect construction sites or work in offices and, eventually, homes.
5. Released in 2003, RoboSapien by WowWee was a walking, talking robot toy that could be easily modified by the owner. It has 67 pre-programmed functions including pick-up, throw, kick, dance and fart.
6. Unveiled in 2000, Honda's Advanced Step in Innovative Mobility (ASIMO) was one of the first robots to walk on two legs and has even played football with President Obama. ASIMO was retired in 2018.
7. Sony's AIBO was a hugely popular robot dog series, designed as companions for adults. It launched in 1999. In 2006, when production ended, AIBO was added to the Carnegie Mellon University Robot Hall of Fame.
8. The General Atomics MQ-1 Predator drone was retrofitted with Hellfire missiles in 2001 and has since been used by the US Air Force and CIA in operations in Afghanistan, Pakistan and Syria.
9. The LEGO MINDSTORMS NXT and EV3 robotics kit were released in 2006 and 2013. They contain a brick-shaped computer, sensors and motors and introduce children to robotics and programming. In 2008 they were welcomed to the Carnegie Mellon University Robot Hall of Fame.
10. The floor-cleaning robot, Roomba, has been vacuuming up homes since its 2002 launch. A third generation model came out in 2007 and is still a popular product today.
11. In 2011, RoboKind developed Milo to support children on the autism spectrum. The cheerful-looking robot, at 61 centimetres (2 feet) tall, helped learners to express empathy and to hone in on emotions.

12. Ekso Bionics, founded in 2005, produces the Ekso GT exoskeleton. Approved by the US Food and Drug Administration (FDA) in 2016, this amazing robotic suit has since allowed stroke patients and people suffering from spinal cord injuries to walk again.

13. Since 2012, Jibo Inc. has been working on creating Jibo, the first social robot for your home. Jibo, which resembles a desk fan, recognises faces, plays music, and syncs with your calendar and other home devices. *Time* magazine rated it the Best Innovation in 2017.

14. Double Robotics produces Double, a 'telepresence robot' (a robot with a video screen display) that can be in places when you can't – ideal for telecommuters, teachers and conferences. They started shipping in 2013.

15. In 2014, FDA approved the DEKA robotic arm 'Luke', nicknamed after Star Wars' Luke Skywalker, as a medical device. Developed from 2008 onwards and produced since 2017, this prosthetic is a mind-controlled device capable of complex functions.

16. SoftBank Robotics, which also owns Boston Dynamics, unveiled its semi-humanoid robot 'Pepper' in 2014. Thanks to its ability to monitor facial expressions and detect emotions, Pepper is used as a receptionist and restaurant host.

17. LG's 'Rolling Bot' came out in 2016 – the ball-shaped camera bot is controlled by mobile phone. It lets users check on their home, play with their cat and communicate virtually through its speaker.

18. Moley Robotics launched in 2015, with the goal of creating the world's first robotic kitchen. Integrated into a standard kitchen, the robotic arms and hands learn from you and can stir and garnish food.

19. The emotional support robot 'Kirobo', at 33 centimetres (13 inches) tall, travelled to the International Space Station in 2013 to join the ISS's first Japanese commander, Koichi Wakata.

20. Launched in 2018, the adorable companion robot 'Buddy', by Blue Frog Robotics, can help with daily tasks at home, such as security, entertaining kids and providing companionship for the elderly.

20 EVOLUTIONS IN GAMING

1. The turn of the century brought with it PlayStation 2 – the bestselling video game console of all time. Since 2000, Sony has sold over 155 million and nearly 4,000 compatible games have been released.
2. The year 2000 also saw the release of the strategic life simulation game, *The Sims*. It wasn't the first of its kind, but it was the most popular. Over several instalments, it became the bestselling computer game ever, and was especially popular with female gamers.
3. A year later, Microsoft entered the gaming arena with the Xbox, and then Xbox 360 and Xbox Live in 2005, which revolutionised online gaming and upped the graphics ante considerably.
4. Games got serious in 2002, with the launch of *America's Army*, the official game of the US Army, which introduced the development of new games to address management and policy issues.
5. Valve made PC gaming cool with the release of its digital video game distribution platform Steam in 2003. Players could download, play and update games online rather than buying discs. In 2017, Steam was averaging 14 million concurrent users per day and hosting over 700 million games.
6. 2004 was the year Nintendo reaffirmed its handheld credentials with the release of the Nintendo DS – a portable gaming system with powerful processors, two screens and multiplayer options.
7. And they went one better in 2006 – they got gamers up and off the sofa with Nintendo Wii and its motion-sensitive controllers, introducing gaming to a much wider market.
8. The year to unleash your inner rock god or goddess was 2007, with Harmonix's *Rock Band* – the game had guitar-shaped controllers to really get into the swing of it.
9. *World of Warcraft* came out in 2004, and in 2008 this Massively Multiplayer Online (MMO) game surpassed the 10 million subscriber barrier.
10. With the launch of the iPhone in 2007 and the Apple App Store in 2008, mobile gaming started to gather momentum. 2009 was the year of *Angry Birds* and *Farmville.*

11. *Minecraft*, the sandbox building game that came out initially in 2009, was one of the first indie games to kick-start a movement – no longer were the big developers the only ones with a piece of the pie.

12. Kids went crazy for 2011's *Skylanders: Spyro's Adventure*. It was the first augmented-reality hit that included plastic figurines that interacted with characters in the game.

13. Thanks to online crowdfunding platforms like Kickstarter, which launched in 2009, game creators and tech developers had a new source of income to get ideas off the ground: the eager gaming community.

14. A wave of new, virtual reality headsets started in 2013 with the release of the DK1 version of Oculus Rift to fellow developers and enthusiasts. A consumer version went on sale in 2016.

15. The highly anticipated release of *Grand Theft Auto V* in 2013 helped propel this controversial game series into the top five most successful series of all time.

16. In 2011, free-to-play (F2P) games overtook premium games for the first time in sales from the Apple store. Developers of these games earn money solely through in-game sales and premium access. One of them, *Crossfire* (2007), became the world's top-grossing game in 2014.

17. The online video streaming service Twitch was acquired by Amazon in 2014. In 2018, it had more than 2.2 million broadcasters and 15 million daily active users.

18. eSports had also grown exponentially in the 2000s. Over 200 million viewers watched the online live streams of the 2018 World Championship final of *League of Legend*. In comparison, 'only' 111 million saw that year's Super Bowl and 163 million the 2018 FIFA World Cup Final.

19. Another F2P hit, which incorporated augmented reality, was *Pokémon Go*. Popular with gamers of all ages, it was 2016's gaming summer hit, with 500 million game downloads between July and September alone.

20. Nintendo's Switch, released in 2017, was the first handheld console to blend mobile phones and game consoles for advanced gaming on the go.

20 Ways Mobile Phones Changed

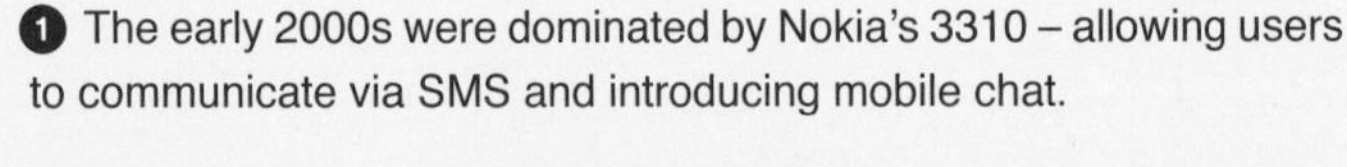

1. The early 2000s were dominated by Nokia's 3310 – allowing users to communicate via SMS and introducing mobile chat.

2. 2000 saw the release of the world's first commercially available mobile camera phone. Sharp's J-SH04 came out on J-Mobile in Japan and had a 0.1-megapixel resolution camera.

3. Japan was ahead of the game – it would be two more years before North America got its first snap-happy cell phone with the Sanyo 5300 from Sprint.

4. The Ericsson R380 was the first device marketed as a 'smartphone'. The Personal Digital Assistant (PDA) device had touchscreen technology (using a stylus) and limited web browsing.

5. The first commercial launch of a 3G network was by NTT DoCoMo in Japan in 2001. A few months later Europe's first commercial network was opened by Telenor.

6. While BlackBerry was previously a data-only device, largely used for two-way paging and email, the BlackBerry 5810 (2000) was the first model to incorporate a phone.

7. T-Mobile's Sidekick was released in 2002 – this phone had a QWERTY keyboard concealed behind a rotating LCD screen. It was one of the first to include a web browser and instant messaging.

8. In 2002, personal digital assistants (PDAs), such as the HP Jornada 928 and Palm's Treo 180, started incorporating wireless voice and data capabilities.

9. Camera phones took a leap forward in 2004 with Motorola's RAZR and its 1.3-megapixel camera. After initial attempts to launch it as upmarket product, it became one of the first mass-marketed, fashionable phones and sold 50 million units over the course of the next two years.

10. The first mobile to incorporate Apple's iTunes music player wasn't an iPhone – it was the Motorola ROKR E1 in 2005. Phones were now music players too.

⓫ The LG Prada (a phone made in collaboration with the high-end fashion house of the same name) was the first to introduce a capacitive touchscreen.

⓬ In 2007, the landscape changed dramatically for the mobile phone market when Steve Jobs introduced the Apple iPhone. This touchscreen-only smartphone revolutionised the user interface with multi-touch gestures.

⓭ Apple launched the online App Store in 2008 with 500 apps. By 2017, it was offering 2.1 million apps to download.

⓮ 2008 saw the release of the HTC Dream slider smartphone – the first to run Google's Android operating system. Customers could use it to browse the web, access Gmail and watch YouTube videos.

⓯ In 2010, a surge in popularity of emojis led to hundreds of emoji characters being encoded in the Unicode Standard version 6.0.

⓰ 2010 was also the year that iPhone announced FaceTime. This videotelephony app enabled iPhone users to make video calls to each other using it.

⓱ The first phone to meet 4G standards was the HTC EVO 4G in 2010. It also had one of the largest touchscreens ever produced, an 8-megapixel camera and mobile hotspot capability.

⓲ After fingerprint scanning was first introduced with the Motorola Atrix in 2011, the 2013 iPhone 5S made this feature available on major US carriers. It became the bestselling phone in that year.

⓳ The first phone using dual-camera technology was the HTC Evo 3D in 2011. The recent global trend, though, started in 2016 with the LG G5 and iPhone 7 Plus. The technology improved mobile phone photography dramatically by taking two simultaneous images with different focal lengths, which were then combined into a finer, sharper and, overall, better result.

⓴ Apple introduced Face ID in 2017 on the iPhone X. It works by projecting a grid of infrared dots onto the user's face, generating a 3D facial map and comparing it with the registered user's face.

20 Tech Start-Ups Worth Big Bucks

1. Between 2005 and 2009, Myspace was the largest social networking site in the world. In 2005 it was bought by News Corporation for $580 million.
2. Uber was founded in 2009 as UberCab by Travis Kalanick and Garrett Camp. After Kalanik once spent $800 hiring a private driver, he wanted to make direct transport cheaper. In 2018, *Reuters* reported the company valued at $120 billion.
3. Airbnb was the brainchild of Brian Chesky, Joe Gebbia and Nathan Blecharczyk after they rented out an air mattress in their apartment in San Francisco, USA, in 2008. By 2018, *Forbes* estimated its worth at $38 billion.
4. The private aerospace company SpaceX was founded in 2002 by PayPal and Tesla founder Elon Musk. At the start of 2019, *Bloomberg* stated its value as $30.5 billion.
5. On-demand transport company Lyft was launched in 2012 and now operates in 400 US cities as well as Canada. Its reported worth is a fraction of rival Uber at $15.1 billion (2018, *CNBC*).
6. Development on Pinterest started in 2009. It now has 250 million active users each month, 81 per cent of whom are women. As a result, the image sharing and social app is worth $13 billion (2018) according to *Forbes*.
7. British food delivery company Deliveroo launched in 2013. The app-based service is now active in 14 countries and, according to *Businessinsider* (2019), worth an estimated $2 billion.
8. When social network Facebook went public in 2012 it was one of the largest and most anticipated IPOs in history. Facebook holds the record for the highest one-day loss of any US stock market company when its shares fell, on 26 July 2018, and erased $120 billion in market value (*Businessinsider*). At the start of 2019 is was worth around $475 billion (*Macrotrends*).
9. A year after Facebook, Twitter also went public. When trading began, the company had an initial valuation of $14 billion. But on their first day on the stock exchange its shares rose in value by over 70 per cent and left Twitter worth $24.4 billion (*CNN*).

10. Swedish music streaming service Spotify was founded in 2006 and launched in 2008. It made its debut on the New York Stock Exchange in 2018 with a value of $30 billion (*Forbes*).

11. In 2017, when Snapchat went public, its disappearing messaging service was being used by 158 million people per day. With stocks soaring by 44 per cent on their first day of trading, *The Guardian* reported Snapchats' initial value increased to $28 billion.

12. Facebook pulled out the big guns to purchase photo- and video-sharing social network Instagram in 2012. It cost them $1 billion.

13. But that was nothing compared to the estimated $19 to $22 billion they paid for Californian-based messaging service WhatsApp in 2014. In 2018 it had a user base of over 1.5 billion people.

14. SurveyMonkey was founded in 1999, and after nearly 20 years of online surveys, it decided to go public in 2018 when it was valued at $2 billion.

15. The birth of her first child in 2008 inspired Actress Jessica Alba to set up the Honest Company. It launched in 2008 selling ethical care products. In 2017 it was valued just shy of $1 billion despite losing its unicorn status (being worth over $1 billion) in 2015.

16. Dating app, Tinder, that lets users choose potential matches by swiping left or right, was valued at $1.35 billion by Bank of America Merrill Lynch in 2015.

17. Digital content creator and broadcaster, Vice Media, started out as a culture magazine in 1994. Significant digital expansion in the late 2000s led to its valuation in 2017 at a reported $5.7 billion (*Forbes*).

18. In 2019, *CNBC* reported that Reddit's value had reached $3 billion. In 2014, the social news and discussion site brought on investors including Snoop Dogg and Jared Leto.

19. Q&A website Quora was created by two former Facebook employees in 2009 and went public a year later. According to *Forbes* it was valued at $1.8 billion in 2017.

20. Microsoft acquired business social network LinkedIn in 2016 for $26.2 billion. It was Microsoft's largest acquisition to date.

20 FASTEST MODES OF TRANSPORT

1. For car lovers, the 2017 Hennessey Venom F5 is the speed superstar. Claiming a top speed of 301 mph (484 kph), it can reach 249 mph (401 kph) in less than 30 seconds.

2. In the same year, the Koenigsegg Agera RS claimed the record as the fastest production car. In three record runs, recorded by the British automotive testing company Racelogic, it managed to achieve an average speed of 277.9 mph (366.8 kph).

3. Hennessey's Venom GT held the previous record, unofficially, with a GPS-verified drive of 270.4 mph (435.2 kph) in 2014 at the Kennedy Space Center.

4. In 2013, Bugatti's Veyron Super Sport claimed the official world's fastest production car title after hitting an average speed of 268 mph (431.3 kph) in tests overseen by Guinness and the German test company TÜV.

5. Debuting in 2004, the magnetic levitation train Shanghai Maglev reaches the Bugatti Veyron's record speeds every day. It hits 267 mph (430 kph) carrying passengers along the 19-mile (30-kilometre) line from Shanghai airport to the city in just seven minutes. The maglev speed record holder is the Japanese Maglev L0 Series. In 2015, it reached 374 mph (over 600 kph) on a test track outside Tokyo.

6. The world's fastest non-maglev train service at present is China's Fuxing Hao CR400AF/BF at 249 mph (400.7 kph). It rolled off the production line in 2015.

7. Italy's Frecciarossa train, or 'Red Arrow', was unveiled during Expo 2015 and travels at speeds up to 220 mph (354 kph).

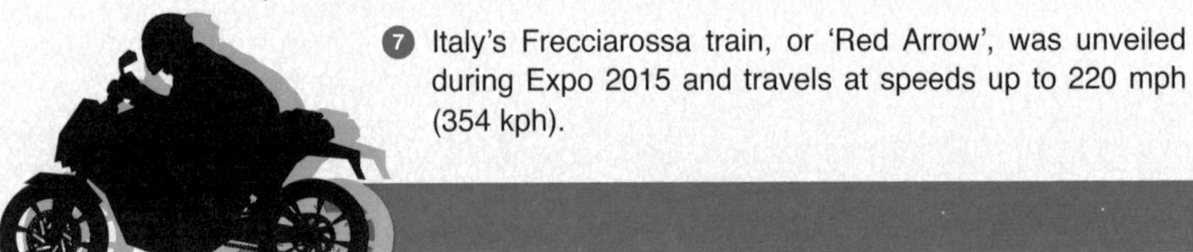

8. 2018 saw the official inauguration of Saudi Arabia's Haramain Western Railway, which connects the country's holy cities. The Haramain can reach 217 mph (349 kph).

9. In 2003, Dodge unveiled the Tomahawk, a superbike capable of a top speed of 420 mph (676 kph). According to reports, only nine people have purchased one so far – at a price of around $555,000 each.

10. The record for the twenty-first-century's fastest production bike to date goes to Kawasaki's Ninja H2R, a bike built for track racing. In 2016, it reached 249 mph (400.7 kph) in only 26 seconds while travelling on a public road over the Osman Gazi Bridge in Turkey.

11. A previous record holder was the MTT Y2K Superbike. Marine Turbine Technologies Inc. (MTT) produced this first-ever turbine-powered motorcycle between 2000 and 2005. Only a little slower than the Kawasaki, but street legal, it reached 227 mph (365 kph).

12. Enjoy your leisure time but still want to go fast? In 2014, Guinness World Records awarded Simon Robin the record for fastest speed achieved in his motorhome, equipped with double bed, sink, stove and toilet. At Elvington Airfield in East Yorkshire, UK, Robin drove 141.3 mph (230 kph).

13. In 2011, Glen Sluter set a new, and still-standing, record for the fastest motorised sofa! At Camden Airport, Australia, his contraption achieved 101.4 mph (167 kph).

14. The world land speed record for a lawnmower is held by Per-Kristian Lundefaret. In 2015 he raced a modified Viking T6 lawnmower at a Norwegian airfield, reaching 133.6 mph (215 kph).

15. Paul Stender from Indianapolis, USA, fitted a fighter plane jet engine into an American school bus that could then travel at 367 mph (590 kph), luckily without any children inside.

16. Despite carrying an additionally fitted 3,000-round machine gun, the FV101 Scorpion managed to become the world's fastest production tank in 2002, travelling at 51 mph (82 kph).

17. In 2013, Australian shipyard Incat unveiled the *Francisco*, which they claimed could travel at 67 mph (108 kph), making it the world's fastest ship.

18. In 2018, Boeing unveiled plans for a new hypersonic 4,000 mph (6,437 kph) jet, which could fly from New York to London in just two hours – faster than Concorde.

19. The world's fastest helicopter, the Eurocopter X^3, broke through the 300 mph barrier with a speed of 303 mph (487.6 kph) in 2013.

20. In 2015, Brad Rowland claimed the title for the world's fastest pontoon boat in his *Tooned In*, which was 25 feet (7.5 metres) long. It travelled at 114 mph (183.5 kph).

20 NEW WAYS TO GET AROUND

1. The London Eye stands at 135 metres (443 feet) high, and when it opened in 2000, it was intended as a temporary structure. It was the world's largest cantilevered observation wheel at the time, only overtaken in 2018 by the 'Bohai Eye' in Weifang, China, at 144.8 metres (475 feet).

2. The Segway HT ('human transporter') launched in 2001. The original two-wheeled personal transporter had three different speed settings with a maximum of 12.5 mph (20.1 kph). On a fully charged battery it could cover 39 kilometres (12.5 miles).

3. In 2003, Inventist released its first successful product, the Aquaskipper – a device that converts the power you generate by up-and-down motion to help you travel on water.

4. When it opened in 2007, the ZipRider at Icy Strait Point in Alaska, USA, which is 1.6 kilometres (1 mile) long, let six riders zip down the mountainside at maximum speeds of 60 mph (96.5 kph).

5. While, at the time of writing, it has yet to be released, the Aero-X hoverbike has been in development since 2008 and has an estimated price tag of $85,000. It's designed to carry two people and can travel at speeds of 45 mph (72.4 kph).

6. Opened in 2008, the Peak 2 Peak Gondola at Whistler-Blackcomb in British Columbia, Canada, has the longest free span between ropeway towers and the highest point above ground of any cable car in the world.

7. In 2009, the YikeBike was unveiled at the international bike trade fair, Eurobike. It's a folding electric bicycle that looks like a miniature penny-farthing, with no chain, pedals or gear box.

8. The compact, seat-less SOLOWHEEL was launched by Inventist in 2011. It's a gyro-stabilised electric unicycle that can reach a maximum speed of 10 mph (16 kph).

9. A helium-filled Hybrid Air Vehicles HAV/Airlander 10 was first test flown in 2012. Once it's in the air, the world's longest aircraft (92 metres/303 feet) can fly for five days without stopping. Originally designed as a military surveillance vehicle, the project was abandoned by the Pentagon in 2013, but resurrected for civilian use in 2015.

10. The Stanserhorn's CabriO cable car in Switzerland opened in 2012. It's the world's first cable car to have a roofless upper deck, so people at the top get 360-degree views.

11 In 2014, General Motors began testing a two-seater urban electric car prototype called En-V. It featured in the futuristic Disney film *Tomorrowland.*

12 Released in 2015, and discontinued in 2016, the Jyrobike was aimed at children learning to ride on two wheels. By using gyroscopes, it eliminates the need for stabilisers to help kids balance.

13 The Lexus SLIDE hoverboard was debuted in an online video in 2015. The wheel-less skateboard uses strong magnets to lift into the air and liquid nitrogen-cooled superconductors. Eat your heart out, Marty!

14 From 2015, shoppers could travel up and down the six floors of the New World Daimaru Department Store in Shanghai using one of the 12 Mitsubishi spiral escalators.

15 In 2017, 30 of the world's super-rich spent £30 million apiece to own a Triton submersible to explore the oceans in style.

16 Richard Branson's Virgin Galactic has been developing commercial spacecraft since 2004. In 2018, *VSS Unity* entered outer space (by US standards) for the first time.

17 It cost $177 to ride the Ras Al Khaimah zip line when it opened in the United Arab Emirates in 2018. At close to 100 mph (160 kph), the experience on the world's longest zip line (2.8 kilometres/1.7 miles) is probably worth every cent.

18 Siemens Mobility's design, called Inspiro, was chosen in 2018 for the new Piccadilly Line cars for the London Underground. Debuting in 2024, they'll have built-in Wi-Fi, air-cooling, LED alerts and driverless capabilities.

19 The Ba Na Hill Cable Car in Vietnam broke four Guinness World Records in 2009, including being the longest single-wire cable car system in the world, stretching over 5 kilometres (more than 3 miles).

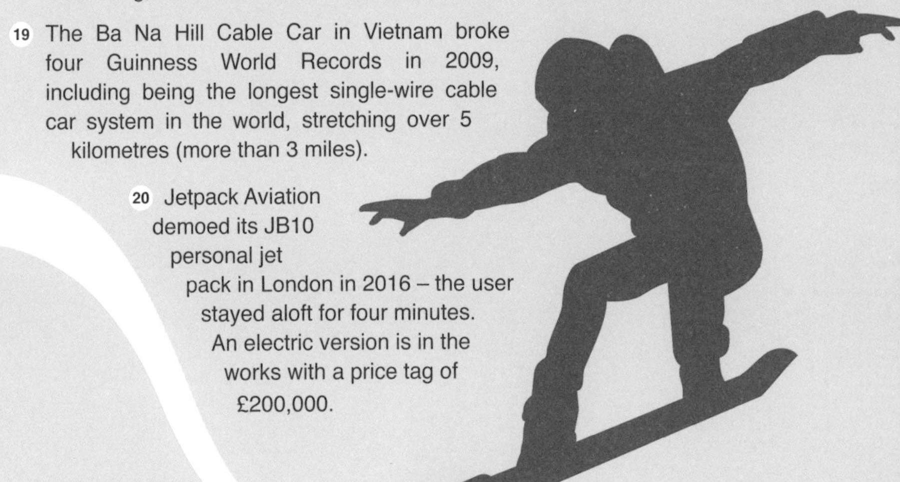

20 Jetpack Aviation demoed its JB10 personal jet pack in London in 2016 – the user stayed aloft for four minutes. An electric version is in the works with a price tag of £200,000.

20 TRIPS IN SPACE

1. American entrepreneur Dennis Tito became the world's first paying tourist to visit the International Space Station (ISS) in 2001, where he spent seven days.

2. 2001 also saw the longest space walk in history so far when NASA astronauts Jim Voss and Susan Helms spent eight hours, 56 minutes performing maintenance work on the ISS.

3. The South African entrepreneur Mark Shuttleworth became the second official space tourist and first South African in space in 2002.

4. On 1 February 2003, tragedy struck when the space shuttle *Columbia* disintegrated as it re-entered the Earth's atmosphere. There were no survivors.

5. China's first 'taikonaut', Yang Liwei, took the nation to space for the first time in 2003 aboard *Shenzhou 5.*

6. After a seven-year journey, the Cassini-Huygens spacecraft has become the first ever to orbit the giant-ringed planet Saturn in 2004. The international space mission saw a collaboration of NASA, the European Space agency (ESA) and the Italian Space Agency (ASI).

7. Scaled Composites won the $10 million X PRIZE in 2004 with *SpaceShipOne*, when it became the first private company to surpass an altitude of 100 kilometres (62 miles).

8. NASA launched the *Discovery* space shuttle in 2005, commanded by Eileen Collins, who performed the first 360-degree pitch manoeuvre.

9. Entrepreneur and scientist Gregory Olsen became the third space tourist in 2005, costing him an estimated $20 million. He conducted several experiments aboard the ISS.

10. The second post-*Columbia* disaster test flight crew from NASA took off successfully aboard *Discovery* on 4 July 2006.

11. In 2007, NASA's *Endeavour* space shuttle transported the organisation's first educator space flyer – teacher-astronaut Barbara Morgan.

12 A couple of months later, the first female commander of the ISS, Peggy Whitson, headed back there with NASA's second female shuttle commander, Pamela Melroy.

13 In 2009, American businessman Charles Simonyi became the first repeat private visitor to space when he paid a second time to fly aboard *Soyuz TMA-14* (his first trip was in 2007).

14 The largest human gathering in space of 13 people took place in 2009 when *Endeavour* docked with the ISS – so far, the record has yet to be beaten.

15 And 2010 saw four women in orbit together for the first time – NASA astronauts Tracy Caldwell Dyson, Stephanie Wilson, Dorothy Metcalf-Lindenburger and Japan's Naoko Yamazaki.

16 Three LEGO mini-figures (of the Roman god Jupiter, his wife Juno and Galileo Galilei) boarded the Juno deep space probe in 2011 on a five-year mission to Jupiter.

17 The space vehicle *Curiosity* made it to the surface of the 'red planet' in 2011 where it has been researching ever since – even finding water on Mars!

18 Red Bull Stratos was a 2012 space diving project. Austrian skydiver Felix Baumgartner jumped to Earth from a helium balloon in the stratosphere in 2012, setting the world record for skydiving at an estimated 39 kilometres (24.2 miles).

19 The huge cost of space travel was significantly reduced in 2015 with the entry of Space X's reusable rocket system.

20 Scott Kelly took part in NASA's One-Year Mission aboard the ISS between 2015 and 2016, spending the highest number of consecutive days – 342 – in space for an American. The longest consecutive space flight ever was done by Valeri Polyakov, who spent nearly 438 days on the former Russian Mir space station.

20 SHOCKING THINGS THAT HAPPENED ON PLANES

1. A British couple took to the skies in 2008 to tie the knot from the wings of two stunt planes. They were wed by a vicar riding the wings of a third.

2. An unfortunate coincidence on a 2008 Ryanair flight caused an emergency landing when a jar of mushroom soup leaked from the overhead lockers onto a man with a mushroom allergy.

3. AirAsia awarded unconditional, complimentary flights for life to a baby born on a two-hour flight from Penang to Kuching in Malaysia in 2009.

4. It was raining maggots on a 2010 US Airways flight when the critters started falling out of an overhead locker. A passenger had brought spoiled meat on board.

5. 2011 saw an embarrassed Gerard Depardieu removed from a flight. After the seat belt sign had been switched on for the take-off, the lavatories were closed. Depardieu tried to urinate into a bottle instead – in front of his fellow passengers.

6. *Snakes on a Plane* became a bit too real in 2012 when a reptile shop owner brought a cobra on board an EgyptAir flight in his hand luggage. It bit him and got out of the bag, causing chaos.

7. One emergency landing at London Gatwick in 2012 was caused after a passenger set fire to his friend's hair as a joke.

8. A Whitney Houston-loving woman was removed from a plane in 2013 after singing 'I Will Always Love You' repeatedly at the top of her voice.

9. A passenger on a 2014 China Airlines flight caused $13,100 worth of damage after landing when he activated the emergency slide in order to get off the plane more quickly.

10. Even more surprising was the United Airlines staff member who took a shortcut down the slide two years later. She was fired.

11. When an American Airlines passenger spotted a weird device taped to the inside of the plane toilet in 2014, they thought it was a bomb. The flight from San Francisco, California, USA, to New York made an emergency landing in Kansas City only to discover that it was in fact a harmless camera disguised as a flash drive.

12 2014 was also the year a woman threw food at staff on a Thomson Airlines flight before removing her prosthetic leg and hurling that at them too.

13 A 2015 flight from Dallas/Fort Worth International Airport (USA) was delayed by an hour when a swarm of more than 1,000 bees took up residence under one of the wings.

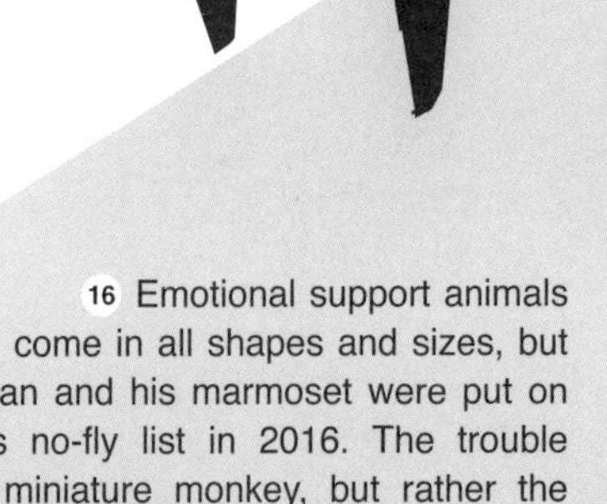

14 On a 2016 flight from the Philippines to South Korea, a door wasn't shut properly on the plane. It took 40 minutes of flight time before anyone noticed.

15 An electronic cigarette exploded on a plane at Hartsfield Jackson Atlanta Airport (USA) in 2016. Luckily, no one was harmed.

16 Emotional support animals come in all shapes and sizes, but a man and his marmoset were put on Frontier's no-fly list in 2016. The trouble was not the miniature monkey, but rather the passenger's failure to produce the correct paperwork. Even more unusual support animals include a miniature Appaloosa horse, and even some turkeys.

17 In 2016, a bird struck a plane flying from New York to Tennessee, USA – the force was so strong it cracked the windscreen.

18 Passport-carrying pet falcons are a common sight on Middle Eastern airlines – in 2017 a viral photo captured more than twenty on the same flight.

19 In 2018, Pope Francis married two cabin crew members during a LATAM Airlines flight over Chile, after learning the church they'd planned to marry in had been destroyed by an earthquake.

20 Also in 2018, a flight from Dubai, UAE, to Amsterdam, Netherlands, had to make an emergency landing after two passengers started fighting about the fact one of them wouldn't stop farting.

20 New Cities to Visit

1. Forest City, Malaysia, is being built on reclaimed land near to Singapore's north-western tip. With space for 700,000 people, it's due for completion in 2035.

2. China is also getting a Forest City – with a 2020 completion date. The environmentally friendly Guangxi Province development will be covered in around one million plants and will produce 914 tonnes (900 tons) of oxygen annually.

3. In 2001, Malaysia's Prime Minister Mahathir declared the new city of Putrajaya a Federal Territory, and nearly all of the country's government ministries had moved there by 2012.

4. Construction started on the new Myanmar capital, Nay Pyi Taw, in 2002 and was completed by 2012. In 2006, a parade of 12,000 military troops marked the city's first public event.

5. In 2017, the Bill Gates investment group (Cascade Investment) invested $80 million to buy 10,117 hectares (25,000 acres) of desert earmarked for the 'Smart City Belmont' project, outside Phoenix, Arizona, USA. The area has been poised for development since the early 1990s, but plans have stalled several times.

6. South Korea's Songdo is still in development, but when finished, the sustainable city will feature smart homes, electric car charging stations and a unique waste collection system.

7. The new grand Kangbashi District in Inner Mongolia became internationally known in 2009 when Al Jazeera reported on its opulent architecture and lack of residents, calling it a 'ghost town'.

8. Sixty-five million cubic metres (2,995 million cubic feet) of sand will eventually become the foundation of Port City, Sri Lanka. Built on land fully reclaimed from the Indian Ocean, this ambitious project will eventually double the size of the existing capital, Colombo. It was first proposed in 2004 and is due to be fully completed in 2041.

9. 2017 saw a groundbreaking ceremony take place at the small fishing village of Duqm, Oman, where the $10.7 billion Sino-Oman Industrial City is being built.

10. With an estimated price tag of $500 billion, Neom in north-west Saudi Arabia had an original phase one completion date of 2025.

11. King Abdullah Economic City, Saudi Arabia, was named for the then-king who announced the project in 2005. The city is the setting for the 2012 Dave Eggers' novel *A Hologram for the King.*

12. Oman's coastal Blue City or Al Madina A'Zarqa was launched in 2007, but the credit crunch brought the project to a grinding halt that, at the time of writing, has yet to get started again.

13. 2018 saw construction start on Gracefield Island, near Lagos, Nigeria on 100 hectares (247 acres) of reclaimed land. The new metropolis will offer luxury accommodation and amenities for the country's elite.

14. Indonesia's Dompak was inspired by Putrajay in Malaysia, but by 2010 only a third of the eco-city's infrastructure had been built using already 75 per cent of the budget.

15. Georgia's Tbilisi Sea New City began construction in 2012. Once completed, its 120,000 square metre (1.3 million square foot) Hualing Tibilisi Sea Plaza will be the largest trade centre in the Caucasus.

16. At the border of China and Kazakhstan is the Chinese city of Horgos, a $3.25 billion new city housing 200,000 people.

17. On the other side of the border is Nurkent, Kazakhstan. So far only a small camp housing 1,200 employees, and their families, of dry port, train station and custom offices, it is set to become a cultural and commercial centre for 100,000 residents by 2035.

18. Xiong'an is currently considered China's No.1 urban project. The mega-city is to be built just over 100 kilometres (62 miles) south of Beijing. Three counties in Hebei Province were declared as 'Xiong'an New Area'. When building started in 2017, local property sales skyrocketed and regulators had to step in.

19. Gauteng province in South Africa is home to five new in-development cities including Waterfall City, which began in 1997.

20. A 2017 deal was struck between Malaysia's government and its Chinese partner to build Robotic Future City for $3.4 billion – a futuristic hub for the robotics industry.

20 UNBELIEVABLE JOURNEYS AROUND THE WORLD

1. Between March 2013 and March 2016, Spanish adventurer Ignacio 'Nacho' Dean became the fifth man to walk around the world. He covered 33,000 kilometres (20,505 miles) in 1,095 days.

2. When British runner Robert Garside arrived in New Delhi in June 2003 he became the Guinness World Record holder for the first person to run around the world.

3. In 2005, Jesper Kenn Olsen from Denmark also completed a round-the-world run. He was the first person to achieve this running in a north–south direction, as opposed to east–west.

4. While raising money for Oxfam, Australian Tom Denniss broke a world record in 2011 when he completed his 26,232 kilometre (16,300 miles) round-the-world run in 622 days.

5. In 2001, British sailor Ellen MacArthur sailed non-stop around the world, single-handedly, in 94 days, 4 hours, 25 minutes making her the female world record holder.

6. A few years later Ellen became the youngest person to be made a Dame when she beat Francis Joyon's subsequent round-the-world record, making it over the finish line in just over 71 days.

7. In 2010, Australian sailor Jessica Watson became the youngest person, at the age of 16, to perform a solo, non-stop, southern hemisphere circumnavigation.

8. American artist Reid Stowe spent 1,152 days at sea between 2007 and 2010 – the longest time spent at sea without touching land or resupplying. His wife had originally joined him but left the voyage after 306 days.

9. The first solar vehicle to circumnavigate the globe was *Tûranor PlanetSolar*, which set off from Monaco with a four-person crew in 2010.

10 Gerry Hughes, a British yachtsman, became the first profoundly deaf person to sail single-handedly around the world, passing the five great capes in 2013.

11 Steve Fossett become the first person to make a solo flight around the world in a balloon. His 10 storey high balloon, named *Spirit of Freedom*, took off from Australia in 2002. He crossed the finishing line after 13 days, having covered 31,266 kilometres (19,430 miles).

12 In 2014, at the age of 19 years, seven months, Matt Guthmiller became the youngest person to complete a global circumnavigation, stopping 23 times in 15 countries.

13 In 2016, Silver Airways captain Wang Zheng became the first Asian woman to fly around the world and the first Chinese person to fly solo around the world.

14 English adventurer Colin Bodill successfully completed the first solo circumnavigation by a microlight in 2000. It took him 99 days.

15 After Guinness World Records updated the rules for a proper circumnavigation, Steve Strange became the first true cycling circumnavigator in 2005, cycling for 276 days.

16 The first woman to do this was British-German cyclist Juliana Buhring, who completed her ride in 2012 after spending 152 days in the saddle.

17 And the fastest cyclist to make it round the globe (in under 80 days!) is Mark Beaumont, who finished his attempt in 2017 after 78 days, 14 hours, 40 minutes of riding.

18 It took Jason Lewis just over 13 years to become the first person to circumnavigate the globe with human power, which allows any human-powered method of travel to be used. The journey included crossing the Atlantic in a wooden pedal-powered boat and rollerblading across America.

19 And the first person to do a similar journey completely solo was Erden Eruç, who travelled by rowboat, bicycle, sea kayak and on foot between 2007 and 2012.

20 Preferring motorised assistance, Kane Avellano circumnavigated the globe on a motorcycle. He was 23 when he completed the ride in 2017, making him the youngest person to do so.

20 Times Rich People Travelled in Style

1. Prince Sultan Bin Fahd of Saudi Arabia commissioned an RV bus with a large lounge, five-star bedrooms and designer finishes throughout.
2. The EC135 Hermès is a luxury helicopter, with handcrafted leather seats and space for four passengers. It has a price tag of $6 million.
3. The Terra Wind RV Amphibious Coach launched in 2012 – the most luxurious way to travel by land *and* by water.
4. The Emperor of Japan asked Toyota to produce four new cars for him. They delivered the Century Royal Limousine with wool cloth upholstery, rice-paper finishing and granite entry steps.
5. In 2013, Rolls-Royce created a specially designed Phantom with a 15-speaker system, picnic compartment and diamond-encrusted fibre-optic ceiling to give the effect of a night sky.
6. The new millennium brought with it the Airbus ACJ319 at a cost of $87 million. It comes with a customisable cabin of approximately 74.3 square metres (800 square feet), optional cinema lounge and luxury king-size bedrooms.
7. For Father's Day 2012, Jay-Z received a $40 million Bombardier Challenger 850 jet from his wife Beyoncé. It has a kitchen, living room and two bathrooms.
8. John Travolta is a qualified pilot and even has his own runways. In 2001, he painted his B707 in original Qantas colours and took it on a tour of 10 Qantas destinations.
9. In 2007, it was announced that Russian billionaire and Chelsea Football Club owner, Roman Abramovich had swapped his Boeing 767 for a $300 million Airbus A380 super-jumbo.
10. In 2011, Rihanna made public transport look cool when she rode the London Underground accompanied by her entourage and bodyguards.

11. In 2017, Emirates unveiled their Boeing 777's brand new interiors, including private first-class cabins with personal lighting and temperature controls.

12. In 2012, the Pope received a Mercedes-Benz M-Class sport utility vehicle with a hydraulic lift and glass-enclosed room, known as the 'Popemobile'. It even has its own oxygen supply.

13. Russian billionaire Andrey Melnichenko spent $450 million having his *Sailing Yacht A* built. With three masts measuring 90 metres (295 feet), it's the world's tallest super-yacht.

14. Global superstars Kim Kardashian and Kanye West were heavily criticised in 2018 when they hired a 660-seater Boeing 747 jet to fly to Japan. It was just them and their entourage on board.

15. In 2013, Kanye also splashed out about $2.4 million on two customised DARTZ Prombon Iron Diamond armoured SUVs to protect his family from fans, landmines and grenades.

16. Before their dramatic split, Angelina Jolie spent $1.6 million in 2012 on a helicopter and flying lessons for her husband Brad Pitt.

17. Rap star Sean 'Puffy' Combs has reportedly spent $900,000 *per week* on luxury yacht rentals for a rather indulgent vacation.

18. While working on *Two and a Half Men*, Ashton Kutcher lived it up in a trailer of 93 square metres (1,000 square feet). With seven plasma TVs, two bathrooms, a kitchen and a conference area, it was worth $2 million.

19. While out and about on the campaign trail, President Obama got comfy in a $1.1 million all-black tour bus. It had tinted windows and was packed with security features.

20. In 2006, the stars of *The Da Vinci Code,* Tom Hanks and Audrey Tautou, rode the Eurostar from London, UK, to Cannes, France, on the longest non-stop high-speed international train journey – 1,421 kilometres (883 miles).

20 Things We Learned About the Universe

1. During the Hubble Space Telescope's 2002 Servicing Mission 3B it detected an object on the Kuiper belt at the edge of our solar system – a dwarf planet Eris, which is bigger than Pluto, leading scientists to question Pluto's planet status.
2. We learned about remote galaxies and how they were much larger than previously predicted. One, discovered in 2016, was the most distant ever seen.
3. In 2006, researchers found evidence that proved the existence of dark matter. While its contents are still a complete mystery, NASA confirmed that they know 68 per cent of the universe is composed from it.
4. The first image of an exoplanet (an extrasolar planet) was taken by Hubble in 2008. It was the same year the telescope found organic molecules on such a planet.
5. We learned more about how stars are born thanks to a photo of star-forming region 'Rho Oph', which revealed new stars peeking out from beneath a blanket of dust.
6. The first discovery of 'buckyballs', football-shaped carbon molecules, took place in 2010. They're the largest molecules known to exist in space and had only previously been observed in the lab.
7. In 2012, Hubble images showed seven primitive galaxies that formed more than 13 billion years ago. The images show the universe when it was less than 3 per cent of its current age.
8. The year 2013 saw astronomers determining the true colour of a planet orbiting another star for the first time. Known as HD 189733b, the planet is a deep azure blue.
9. In the same year we learned that water vapour was erupting off the surface of Europa, one of Jupiter's moons – only the second moon in the solar system known to have water vapour.
10. In 2014, astronomers witnessed the never-before-seen break-up of an asteroid in the asteroid belt. It fragmented into as many as ten smaller pieces.

⑪ A team of scientists were able to create a detailed map of an exoplanet's atmosphere for the first time in 2014, tracing the amount of water it contains.

⑫ In 2017, the first-ever confirmed interstellar object visited our solar system. Called 'Oumuamua' the asteroid had a bizarre cigar-like shape and was originally mistaken for a comet.

⑬ That same year scientists discovered that a few small asteroids orbiting Mars were made of the same material, suggesting they could have been from the core of a long-lost planet. They contained material found only inside planets the size of Mercury or Mars.

⑭ In 2017, we also learned that dwarf planet Haumea, which orbits around Neptune, has a ring (making it the only dwarf planet to have one) and twin moons, and it rotates once every 3.9 hours.

⑮ On the gassy Kepler-13Ab, an exoplanet nearly three times the size of Jupiter, sunscreen, or at least the active ingredient in sunscreen, titanium oxide, falls from the sky like snow.

⑯ Researchers think that, similarly to these sunscreen snowstorms, it could be raining diamonds on Uranus and Neptune. In 2017, under simulated conditions, they proved it was possible.

⑰ NASA intentionally smashed Deep Impact into a comet in 2005 to analyse the ingredients of our solar system's 'soup'. Ingredients have since been identified as silicates, clay, carbonates, iron-bearing compounds and aromatic hydrocarbons… delicious!

⑱ We got a closer look at the largest known ring around Saturn in 2017 – the ring starts 6 million kilometres (3.7 million miles) from the planet and is 20 times thicker than Saturn's diameter.

⑲ In 2018, two of the most distant supermassive black holes were detected by NASA's Spitzer Space Telescope, helping us to understand the roots of our universe.

⑳ Perhaps most excitingly, 2017 was the year Spitzer revealed the first-known system of seven Earth-size planets around a single star, with three located in the habitable zone where life could potentially flourish.

20 AWESOME ARCHAEOLOGICAL FINDS

1. In 2015, Nicholas Reeves' laser scans of Tutankhamun's tomb in the Valley of the Kings, Egypt, revealed two hidden chambers, sealed for millennia.

2. A virtually unknown culture, thought to have existed 1,000 years ago, was discovered in the eastern Mosquitia region of the Honduran rainforest in 2015.

3. In 2013, cavers in South Africa stumbled across the remains of more than 15 individuals – they turned out to be a new species in humankind's evolutionary history – *Homo naledi.*

4. In 2010, four burial grounds in Jamestown, Virginia, USA, were the site of an archaeological dig. There researchers identified the remains of the first major English church building in North America, dating back to 1608.

5. What was believed to be the remains of a puppy, found in the 1980s in a 2,000-year-old Native American burial ground in the United States, were re-examined in 2015 and found to be those of a wild bobcat – the first discovered burial of its kind.

6. Two 6,000-year-old skeletons were found in 2007 near Mantua, Italy – they had their arms wrapped around each other and their legs intertwined.

7. A warrior's tomb found in 2015 in the south-western Peloponnese was the biggest Greek archaeological discovery in decades. It contained 1,400 objects, including precious jewellery.

8. 2015 was also the year that the early eighteenth-century Spanish galleon, the *San Jose*, was found off the coast of Cartagena, Colombia, containing an estimated $1 billion to $17 billion worth of gems and metal.

9. In 2016, scientists used electrical resistivity to discover a third pyramid hidden inside the two known pyramids of El Castillo, in Chichén Itzá, Mexico, constructed between 600 and 800 CE.

10. A 2016 CT scan of a small, cedar, Egyptian coffin at Cambridge's Fitzwilliam Museum, UK, found it to contain a mummified foetus, thought to be the youngest mummy ever found.

11. The 11 caverns at Qumran near Israel and Palestine (unearthed in the 1940s and 1950s) contained the historically significant Dead Sea Scrolls. In 2017, a twelfth cave was found.

12. In 2012, the excavation of a car park in Leicester, UK, unearthed a skeleton. DNA and forensic analysis enabled scientists to determine that the bones belonged to King Richard III.

13. After years of exploration the 1,700-year-old Roman city of Neapolis was found off the coast of Tunisia. It was submerged after a tsunami in the fourth century.

14. A collaborative team of marine scientists, archaeologists and volunteers located two American World War Two B-25 bombers in the waters off Papua New Guinea in 2017.

15. A vast Viking camp on the banks of the River Trent in Lincolnshire, UK, was uncovered in 2017. Thousands of Vikings lived there in the late ninth century as they prepared to invade England.

16. In 2007, early squash seeds were uncovered in buried house floors in the Andean Ñanchic Valley in Peru, helping archaeologists to date agricultural lifestyles in the region.

17. Radiocarbon dating of a body discovered in Ireland's Cashel Bog in 2013 found it to be the oldest fleshed bog body in Europe, predating the title holder by 600 years.

18. New chemical analyses conducted in 2012 on a 24,000-year-old notched, wooden stick from South Africa's Border Cave revealed traces of poisonous castor beans. This is considered to be the earliest evidence of humans using poison.

19. A 2004 dig on the Indonesian island of Sumbawa revealed the first evidence of the Kingdom of Tambora, which was destroyed by a volcanic eruption in 1815.

20. Further examination of the Xianrendong Cave in Jiangxi Province, China, revealed what archaeologists now believe to be the oldest known pottery in the world, up to 20,000 years old.

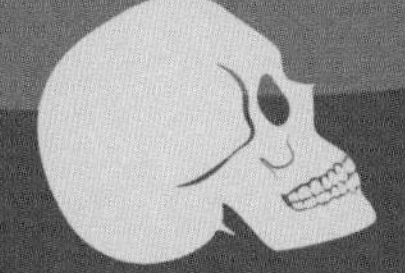

20 Pioneering Surgical Procedures

1. In 2000, the Da Vinci Surgical System was cleared by the US Food and Drug Administration (FDA). It is a robotic piece of equipment designed to help perform minimally invasive surgeries, including hysterectomies and prostate removals. By 2017 there were over 4,000 Da Vinci systems in use around the world.

2. Deep Brain Stimulation (DBS) – the application of an electrical pulse to specific brain nuclei – has been approved for the treatment of the tremors associated with Parkinson's Disease since 1999. However, developments in implant control technology mean that, in the case of the device from Abbott's called the Infinity DBS System, patients can control DBS wirelessly, by smartphone.

3. In 2014, the first baby was born to a woman who had received a uterus transplant. The transplant was performed by Dr Mats Brännströn and a team at the University of Gothenburg in Sweden.

4. And that same year two other Swedish women gave birth to children after undergoing womb transplants that they had received from their own mothers.

5. Four years later, in 2018, at the Hospital das Clínicas at the University of São Paulo School of Medicine in Brazil, the first baby was born to a woman who had received a uterus from a deceased donor.

6. Isabelle Dinoire was the first person to receive a partial face transplant, a triangle of face tissue, in 2005 after she had been mauled when attacked by a dog. The surgery was performed in Amiens, France.

7. Three years later, in 2008, Pascal Caler was the recipient of what his doctors referred to as the world's first successful 'almost full face' transplant. The surgery lasted 20 hours.

8. And, in 2010, the world's media reported the first full face transplant had been carried out by a team of Spanish doctors to a man who was injured in a shooting incident. It was believed to be the most complex of all previous facial transplants, including all of the face and some bone.

9. Unfortunately, the recipient of the world's first double leg transplant, carried out in 2011, had to have his new legs amputated two years later when an unrelated illness forced the man to stop taking his anti-rejection medication.

10. The surgeons who performed the double leg transplant, led by Pedro Cavadas, also performed the world's first double hand transplant in 2006.

11. A revolution in cancer treatment occurred in 2008 when French neurosurgeons destroyed a brain tumour on a conscious patient using keyhole laser surgery.

12. Sherrie Walter got a new ear in 2012 after she had suffered from a serious bout of skin cancer. Johns Hopkins surgeons in Baltimore, Maryland, USA, grew the ear in the woman's own forearm from her own rib cartilage.

13. Similarly, Chinese surgeons in Imperial College, Fuzhou, grew a replacement nose on a patient's forehead in 2013.

14. Danielle Press was severely injured in a boating accident in 2013. One month later she had pioneering surgery at the Miller School of Medicine, Miami, Florida, USA, where surgeons performed the world's first nerve graft to repair her sciatic nerve.

15. A technological leap took place in 2013 when surgeons from the University of Alabama, USA, used a virtual augmented reality technology and Google Glass to perform a shoulder replacement surgery.

16. In 2014, South African surgeons announced they had performed the first successful penis transplant on a 21-year-old recipient who was left with a one centimetre penis after a botched circumcision.

17. Four years later, surgeons at Johns Hopkins Hospital went one better, successfully transplanting a penis and scrotum in the first surgery of its kind. The patient had suffered devastating injuries while serving in the war in Afghanistan.

18. In 2015, an American man received the world's first skull and scalp transplant after parts of his own were destroyed by cancer treatment. He also received a new pancreas and kidney during the procedure.

19. In 2016, Johns Hopkins became the first US hospital to perform HIV-positive to HIV-positive organ transplants: a liver and a kidney.

20. A pioneering software system, being trialled in 2018 at University College London Hospital, created a 3D map of a patient's brain to aid surgeries removing parts of the brain of epilepsy sufferers.

20 BIG MEDICAL DEVELOPMENTS

1. The early part of the twenty-first century saw a huge drop, by more than 40 per cent, in the number of deaths from heart disease, thanks to the long-term effects of new statins drugs.

2. In 2002, the Food and Drug Administration (FDA) in the United States approved the first rapid HIV diagnostic test kit, allowing hospitals to provide 99.6 per cent accurate results in just 20 minutes.

3. The completion of the Human Genome Project in 2003 has led to cancer genome sequencing being integrated into medical care facilities and has helped scientists understand genes involved in diabetes, eczema and leukaemia.

4. Minimally invasive and robotic surgical techniques, such as kidney transplants conducted through a single incision in a patient's navel, first performed at the Cleveland Clinic, Ohio, USA, in 2007, have improved recovery times substantially.

5. In 2015, Massachusetts General Hospital and Harvard Medical School in the United States got a step closer to creating a bioengineered human, paving the way for less reliance on organ donation. They regenerated functional human heart tissue by inserting heart muscle cells generated from stem cells of one person into a donor heart of another, which was stripped of all components that would prompt the body to reject it.

6. The digitisation of information through electronic health records has had a huge impact on patient care. In 2011, the European Commission announced it wanted all Europeans to be able to access their online medical records anywhere in Europe by 2020.

7. In 2013, an American company called Second Sight started making a bionic eye that uses a camera built into glasses to be worn by the user. The camera transmits electrical messages to the retinal implant.

8. In 2015, scientists discovered the first new antibiotic in nearly 30 years. *Teixobactin* has been trialled in mice to treat tuberculosis and septicaemia.

9. And in the future, new eye drops created by the University of California in 2015 might be able to melt away the amyloids that lead to cataracts, avoiding surgery for patients.

10. 3D-printed body parts have started to become viable options. In 2013 Cornell University, New York State, printed an outer ear; and a company called Organovo, based in California, USA, is committed to printing human livers by 2020.

11. Gene therapy, such as that used to cure a teenage boy of sickle cell disease in 2017, has been used to build skin, restore sight and increase blood-clotting proteins.

12. Scientists are discovering how the mix of bacteria or microbes in our digestive system affect our brain functions. A 2013 study on mice with lower levels of *Bacteroides fragilis* showed a tendency towards autism.

13. Studies in 2018 showed how new faecal transplant treatments for conditions such as Parkinson's disease and irritable bowel syndrome can replace common gut bacteria in those who have had complications after prolonged use of antibiotics.

14. In 2013, Sofosbuvir was approved for medical use in the United States for the treatment of Hepatitis C, a disease that causes 12,000 deaths per year.

15. Research into synthetic cells has progressed rapidly since the first ones were created in 2010. In 2017, Israeli researchers developed synthetic cells that could produce an anti-cancer protein to kill surrounding breast cancer cells.

16. The Food and Drug Administration in the United States approved Medtronic's MiniMed 670G in 2016. The artificial pancreas measures the wearer's blood glucose and delivers insulin through an abdomen pump – a life-changing gadget for those with type-1 diabetes.

17. A procedure using mitochondrial transfer to create a healthy baby that would have otherwise suffered from the fatal Leigh syndrome, took place in 2016. The procedure combines the nucleus of an egg from one parent, inserted into the egg of another, and fertilised by the father's sperm.

18. In 2016, the FDA approved a buprenorphine implant for the treatment of opioid addiction. It provides a constant, low-level dose to the patient as part of a treatment programme, removing the need to remember to take a pill.

19. The first human papilloma virus (HPV) vaccine became available in 2006, helping to prevent infection caused by certain types of the virus, which can cause cervical cancer. By 2017, 71 countries included it in their routine vaccinations for girls.

20. In 2015, the US National Center for Health Statistics (NCHS) reported that long-acting reversible contraceptives had gained popularity because of their effectiveness in preventing unwanted pregnancies. Their use increased nearly five-fold among women aged 15 to 44 years from 2002 to 2013.

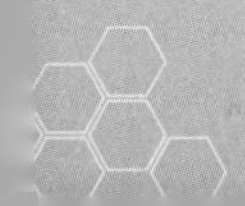

20 NEW SPECIES

1. *Malo kingi*, an Irukandji jellyfish, was officially recognised in 2007. It's the second known species of the *Malo* genus and was named after Robert King who died after being stung by the species off the Queensland coast in Australia.

2. A new species of rhinoceros beetle was discovered in 2007 called *Megaceras briansaltini*. It had a unique horn that gave it a similar appearance to the animated character Dim in *A Bug's Life*.

3. Named in honour of the *Microbacterium* genus researcher Dr Kazunori Hatano, *Microbaterium hatanonis*, an extremophile bacterium ('extremophile' meaning that they can survive in extreme environments) found in hairspray, was discovered in 2008.

4. Unique for its shell's four different coiling axes, the most for any known gastropod, the discovery of *Opisthostoma vermiculum* in 2008 was a new stage in science's understanding of evolutionary shell-twisting.

5. 2008 was also the year a caffeine-free coffee species from Cameroon was discovered. *Coffea charrieriana* is the first caffeine-free species to be found in Central Africa.

6. With its American-football-sized pitchers (giant hollow bulbs), the carnivorous *Nepenthes attenboroughii* is a plant native to the Philippine island of Palawan and was named in honour of naturalist Sir David Attenborough in 2009.

7. *Danionella Dracula* were identified in 2009. The males of these freshwater fish have canine-like fangs that they use to fight with other males.

8. In 2010, researchers discovered the rather unattractive Louisiana Pancake Batfish (*Halieutichthys intermedius*) off the Gulf of Mexico.

9. Known to local hunters but only found by biologists in 2010, in the Northern Sierra Madre Forest on the Philippine island of Luzon, the forest monitor lizard (*Varanus bitatawa*) can grow up to 2 metres (6.5 feet) in length.

10 The Wandering Leg Sausage (*Crurifarcimen vagans*), a form of millipede, measures 16 centimetres (6.3 inches) and was found in 2011 living in decaying wood in Tanzania's Eastern Arc Mountains.

11 Newly known to science and seen for the first time in captivity in 2007, the lesula (*Cercopithecus lomamiensis*) was only the second species of African monkey found in 28 years. This new species was confirmed in 2012.

12 A tiny new frog, called *Paedophryne amanuensis*, was discovered in Papua New Guinea, in 2012. It measures just 7 millimetres (0.275 inches) and claimed the title of being the smallest living vertebrate.

13 The aptly named Tinkerbell Fairyfly (*Tinkerbella nana*) is among the smallest known insects. It was found in 2013 in Costa Rica and measures just 250 micrometres, 2.5 times the width of a human hair.

14 The fictional-sounding Kaweesak Dragon Tree (*Dracaena kaweesakii*) grows on limestone outcrops, and can reach a height of up to 12 metres (30 feet). It has sword-shaped leaves and cream-coloured flowers and was identified in 2013.

15 Discovered in 2014, the *Torquigener albomaculosus* is a pufferfish, the males of which create geometric spawning nests on the sea floor to attract females off the coast of Amami-Ōshima island.

16 Belonging to the giant stick family, *Phryganistria tamdaoensis* is a stick insect that is 23 centimetres (9 inches) long. It was found in 2014 in the Tam Dao National Park in north Vietnam.

17 In 2015, the Galapagos giant tortoise, *Chelonoidis donfaustoi,* was considered to be a genetic variation of the known species *C. porteri.* It was named in honour of a park ranger.

18 Believed to be the first new species of plant discovered in 2015 in photos posted on Facebook, *Drosera magnifica* is the largest sundew in the New World, growing to 123 centimetres (48 inches).

19 Grown inside a spiky shell, *Solanum ossicruentum* is an Australian tomato that appears to bleed when it's cut open before drying into a bony state. It was named by a group of seventh-grade science students from Pennsylvania, USA, in 2016.

20 A small and slender rat found only on Sulawesi Island in Indonesia was discovered in 2016. *Gracilimus radix* (*radix* is Latin for root) is different to its strictly carnivorous relatives, choosing to sometimes feed on roots of trees.

20 DISEASES THAT HAD AN IMPACT

1. In late 2002, the coronavirus SARS (severe acute respiratory syndrome) first infected people in China. Within a few weeks it had spread to 37 countries through air travel, infecting 8,000 people.

2. The HIV virus that causes AIDS continues to be a big global killer. In 2017, 36.9 million people were living with HIV/AIDS.

3. Although malaria is a preventable and curable disease, in 2017 an estimated 219 million people worldwide were infected by it and 435,000 died. Over 90 per cent of cases occur in the African region.

4. The twenty-first century has seen a significant drop in the tuberculosis death rate, but it is still one of the top ten causes of death worldwide. In 2017, 1.6 million people died from the disease.

5. 2015 saw a large outbreak of the Zika virus infection in Brazil, which soon spread to 86 countries. A link was quickly made between the disease in pregnant women and microcephaly.

6. 2009 was the year when a new strain of H1N1 first infected humans. Over four months the influenza virus spread from California, in the United States, to over 70 countries.

7. Nigeria faced its largest ever outbreak of Lassa fever in 2018, with 134 deaths between January and September that year. The viral haemorrhagic illness occurs largely in West Africa.

8. The Ebola outbreak of 2014–2016 was the largest and most complex since the virus was first discovered. In Sierra Leone, Liberia and Guinea alone there were over 11,000 deaths.

9. Human monkeypox appeared for the first time outside the African continent in 2003, when cases were confirmed in the US.

10. In 1999, the West Nile virus (WNV) was first identified outside the Eastern Hemisphere. The virus can cause West Nile fever, a potentially fatal neurological disease. By 2010, over three million people were infected in the US and other locations along bird migration routes. The virus is spread by mosquitoes feeding from bird blood.

11. In 2011, Rinderpest, a cattle disease that once ravaged herds across Asia, Europe and Africa, became the second infectious disease, after smallpox in humans, to be eradicated.

12. The Chikungunya virus typically occurs in Africa, Asia and the Indian subcontinent, however a major outbreak in 2015 saw over 1.3 million suspected cases recorded across the Caribbean Islands, Latin America and the United States.

13. In 2014, there was an outbreak of Marburg virus disease in Angola. With a high death rate, many people were suspicious of health workers and refused treatment. Of the 252 reported cases, 227 resulted in death.

14. Despite smallpox being eradicated in 1980, in 2014 a Food and Drug Administration (FDA) lab in Maryland, USA, discovered six vials of smallpox from 1954 in a cold storage room. Centers for Disease Control and Prevention (CDC) destroyed the virus the following year.

15. Cholera is a diarrhoeal infection with up to four million cases per year. In 2017 the Global Task Force on Cholera Control launched a strategy with the aim of reducing cholera deaths by 90 per cent by 2030.

16. Since the late 1970s, there have been severe Rift Valley Fever (RVF) outbreaks across Africa, but after infected livestock was traded to Saudi Arabia and Yemen in 2000, RVF spread there too, with over 200 deaths reported.

17. The Eliminate Yellow Fever Epidemics Strategy launched in 2017. The unprecedented initiative saw 50 partners working together to support 40 countries. More than one billion people will be protected by 2026.

18. The first identification of the Nipah virus as a cause of encephalitis (brain inflammation) was reported in 2001. Bangladesh faces outbreaks of Nipah virus infection every year, usually in the winter; and in 2018 there was an outbreak in Kerala, India, where 17 deaths were recorded.

19. While it's easily treated nowadays with antibiotics, between 2010 and 2015 there were over 3,000 reported cases of the Plague worldwide, including 584 deaths. In the fourteenth century, the Plague caused over 50 million deaths.

20. 2012 was the year MERS-CoV (Middle East respiratory syndrome coronavirus) was first identified in Saudi Arabia. In the years since, 27 other countries have reported cases.

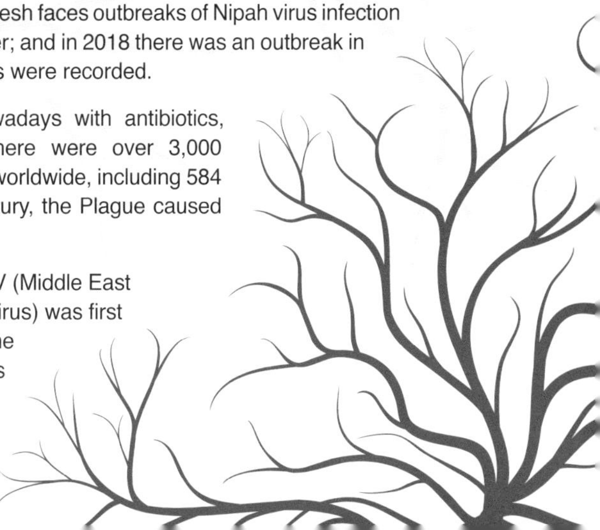

20 Energetic New Ideas

1. In 2013, a new deal was announced that would capture waste heat from the London Underground tunnels to help warm 700 homes in Islington, London.

2. Since 2007, smuggled alcohol seized at customs in Sweden has been converted into biogas to fuel the country's public transport system.

3. In 2017, Japanese diaper producer Unicharm developed a technology to generate electricity from the waste water produced when recycling disposable diapers.

4. The world's first sustainable nightclub popped up in Rotterdam, the Netherlands, in 2008. Its dance floor utilises piezoelectric harvesting technology, converting kinetic energy into electrical energy.

5. In 2010, Israeli company Innowattech planned to install piezoelectric pads on the country's railways to generate enough electricity to power signals, lights and track mechanisms.

6. In 2008, Japan passed a 'Basic Space Law', which established space solar power as a key national goal. A massive solar array floating above the planet beaming wireless electricity to Earth might not be too far in the future.

7. In 2010, Japan's Aerospace Exploration Agency launched IKAROS – the first spacecraft to utilise solar-sailing as its main form of propulsion. Solar wind could also be harnessed for Earth-based energy.

8. With jellyfish populations soaring, Swedish researchers reported in 2010 that they have started extracting the jellyfishes' green fluorescent protein (GFP) to create biofuel cells for nanodevices.

9. The commercial sale of algal biofuels began in 2012. Hailed as a future alternative to fossil fuels, the production of algal biofuels has not yet been sufficiently commercially viable to replace oil in the nearer future.

10. In 2007, Hong Kong's California Fitness gyms introduced step, cycling and cross-training machines that convert energy burned by users into energy for power lighting as well as to help power the machines. Financial mismanagement led to a closure of all outlets in 2018.

11 Launched in 2009, the Pedal-A-Watt stationary bike uses your pedal power to generate energy. An average rider can generate enough electricity in an hour to power a light bulb for a day.

12 In 2001, EnviroMission proposed building a solar updraught tower 792.5 metres (2,600 feet) tall, using a translucent football-field-sized sloping canopy to convert the sun's energy to electricity.

13 In 2008, David Albers, a lifelong dairy farmer, and Pacific Gas and Electric unveiled their Vintage Dairy Biogas Project to convert methane from the manure of Mr. Albers' 5,000 cows into biogas, which is then pumped through the pipeline to power plants.

14 Late 2011 saw the first offshore floating wind farm, situated 349 kilometres (217 miles) off the coast of Portugal, go live. Its 2-megawatt turbine is bolted onto a triangular floating platform.

15 MS *Beluga Skysails* became the first container ship to use auxiliary kite power on a voyage from Germany to Venezuela in 2008. It cut its diesel costs by up to 15 per cent.

16 Richard Handl took energy matters into his own hands when he built a nuclear reactor in his kitchen in 2011 after acquiring all the parts for $950 online. He was arrested after contacting Sweden's nuclear power agency to ask about the legality of his project, but later released and ordered to pay a fine.

17 The University of Nevada, Reno, USA, started researching whether coffee oil could be a feedstock for biodiesel in 2009.

18 A 2007 article by MIT (Cambridge, USA) engineering professor William F. Schreiber proposed launching a fleet of mirrored balloons into orbit. The mirrors could be adjusted to focus solar energy to receiving stations on Earth.

19 In 2014, the German company Sunfire developed a futuristic machine to convert water and CO_2 into fuel, which can take the form of diesel, petrol or kerosene.

20 A self-adjusting tidal turbine produced by researchers at Brown University, Providence, USA, was able to tap into rivers and tides in order to generate electricity. An onboard computer allows it to respond to its environment in real time.

20 DINOSAUR DISCOVERIES

1. In 2000, the Judith River Dinosaur Institute, Montana, USA, found a 77-million-year-old mummified *Brachylophosaurus canadensis*, complete with dinosaur skin. They nicknamed him 'Leonardo' after some nearby graffiti, which read 'Leonard Webb loves Geneva Jordan 1916'.

2. The *Santanaraptor*, discovered near Rio de Janeiro, Brazil, in 2000, was thought to be a descendant of *Tyrannosaurus rex*.

3. It was also the year a *Microraptor*, the smallest theropod dinosaur ever found, with its feather structures intact, was discovered in Liaoning Province, China.

4. Egyptian palaeontologists working in the Bahariya Oasis, Egypt, unearthed the remains of one of the largest dinosaurs ever found in 2001. They named it *Paralititan stromeri*, meaning 'tidal giant'.

5. The species *Nothronychus mckinleyi* was discovered in New Mexico in 2001. It was 3.66 metres (12 feet) tall and is a strange, sloth-like plant-eater with a beak, a long neck and short stumpy legs.

6. The 2004 discovery of the well-preserved pelvis and pelvic fins of 375-million-year-old transitional species *Tiktaalik roseae* in Canada helped reveal the evolution of hind legs, which actually began as hind fins.

7. Unearthed in Argentina in 2000 and named in 2007, *Futalognkosaurus dukei* is one of the most complete giant dinosaurs ever found.

8. In 2009, fossils of Titanoboa, a giant snake, 15.2 metres (50 feet) long and weighing 1,134 kilograms (2,500 pounds), were found in coal mines in La Guajira, Colombia. The snake was so big it could have swallowed a crocodile whole without showing a bulge.

9. Researchers at the University of Utah, USA, discovered *Asilisaurus kongwe* in 2007. The species, an archosaur, shares many characteristics with dinosaurs but lived at least 10 million years before the oldest known species.

10. In 2011, the perfectly preserved top half of a new dinosaur, *Borealopelta markmitchelli*, complete with scaly skin was accidentally found by a mine excavator operator in Alberta, Canada.

11. In 2012, a collection of fossils at Harvard, which came from southern Africa in the 1960s, revealed the existence of *Pegomastax africanus*, a fanged plant-eater smaller than a cat.

12. Chinese palaeontologists discovered the snaggle-toothed *Guidraco venator* (Chinese and Latin for 'ghost dragon hunter') in 2012. The meat-eating pterosaur fossil was thought to be 120 million years old.

13. In 2013, researchers at the University of Toronto in Canada unveiled a new species of bone-headed dinosaur called *Acrotholus audeti*, discovered in southern Alberta. Its dome-shaped skull might have been used to headbutt other dinosaurs.

14. In 2013, the University of Alberta, Canada, published a study that concluded that small, flightless oviraptors had flexible feathered tails that they used to attract a mate.

15. In 2012, researchers at the University of Washington in the United States revealed that upper arm bone and vertebrae found in Tanzania belonging to *Nyasasaurus parrintoni* might be the oldest dinosaur fossils found yet – 243 million years old.

16. Fossils from an unknown dinosaur weighing about two tons were overlooked for decades at London's Natural History Museum – until 2004 when they were cleaned up, studied and the creature was named *Spinops sternbergorum*.

17. In 2012, it was reported that a 150-million-year-old fossil of a baby *Sciurimimus albersdoerferi* was the first evidence of feathered theropod dinosaurs not closely related to birds. Found in the limestones of northern Bavaria (Germany), it indicated that the whole body was covered with feathers.

18. The largest feathered dinosaur was discovered that same year too in China – *Yutyrannus* weighed about one ton, was a distant cousin of the Tyrannosaurus rex and had a coat of feathers.

19. A new horned species of dinosaur was named by Canadian scientists in 2013. The *Xenoceratops foremostensis*, meaning 'alien horned-face' lived 80 million years ago and predates Triceratops.

20. In 2016, the tail of a 99-million-year-old dinosaur, including bones, soft tissue and feathers, was found fully preserved in amber from Myanmar. Researchers believe it belonged to a young coelurosaur.

20 VOLCANIC ERUPTIONS

1. The most devastating volcanic eruption of 2002 took place in DR Congo when Mount Nyiragongo erupted: 400,000 people were evacuated, and around 250 people died from building collapses and asphyxiation.
2. Lucasfilm captured footage of the 2002–2003 eruption of Sicily's Mount Etna, when a huge column of ash was thrown up from the volcano. The footage was used in *Star Wars: Episode III*.
3. In 2004, Manam, a volcanic island off Papua New Guinea's mainland, erupted, forcing 9,000 inhabitants to evacuate.
4. Alaska, in the United States, was the location for a 2008 volcanic eruption when Okmok Caldera exploded without warning. It was the volcano's largest eruption since the thirteenth century.
5. In 2010, a series of small volcanic eruptions of Eyjafjallajökull in Iceland caused nearly a week of severe disruption to air travel across western and northern Europe.
6. That same year Central Java's Mount Merapi in Indonesia started a series of eruptions, resulting in dangerous lava flows. Over 350,000 people were evacuated and approximately 350 people were killed.
7. When Iceland's most active volcano, Grímsvötn, erupted in 2011 it was the country's largest volcanic event for 50 years.
8. Despite being dormant for 51 years, Chile's Puyehue-Cordón Caulle volcano complex erupted in 2011, causing 3,500 people to be evacuated and affecting air travel across the Southern Hemisphere.
9. 2011 also saw a major volcanic eruption of the Nabro stratovolcano in Eritrea. Although exact numbers are uncertain, it's believed 31 people died as a result of the earthquake and thousands more were affected.
10. In 2017, members of a BBC crew were filming in the area when Mount Etna, Italy, experienced a phreatomagmatic eruption – caused when magma hits water (or snow). Six people were taken to hospital.

⑪ Indonesia's Mount Sinabung has seen repeated eruptions since 2013. When ash spewed into the atmosphere in 2010, it marked the volcano's first sign of activity in over four centuries.

⑫ Sinabung is one of 129 active Indonesian volcanoes. It had a deadly eruption in 2016, killing seven people who were farming in the region's 'red zone' at the time.

⑬ An area about 500 kilometres (311 miles) in diameter was affected in 2014 when Kelud in East Java, Indonesia, erupted. Only a few fatalities were reported.

⑭ The same could not be said of the 2014 eruption of Japan's Mount Ontake, which claimed the lives of 63 people. It was the deadliest volcanic eruption in the country for over a century.

⑮ Of Chile's 90 active volcanoes, Calbuco is considered one of the top three most potentially dangerous – 4,000 people had to be evacuated when it erupted in 2015.

⑯ Russia's Kamchatka Peninsula is home to some 300 volcanoes. In 2017, the Kambalny volcano, at 2,165 metres (7,103) feet high, became active for the first time in nearly 250 years.

⑰ Guatemala faced its deadliest volcanic eruption in 45 years, when in June 2018 Volcán de Fuego erupted. Three months later the death toll was reported at 165, with 260 people still missing and 2,900 displaced. The volcano erupted anew in October 2018.

⑱ Ecuador's isolated Reventador volcano is situated in the eastern Andes. Its largest historical eruption took place in 2002, with a plume reaching a height of 17 kilometres (10.6 miles).

⑲ In 2018, Hawaii's (USA) Kīlauea – the most active of the island's volcanoes – erupted causing a month-long closure to the Volcanoes National Park and destroying the island's largest freshwater lake.

⑳ At the end of 2018, Indonesia's Anak Krakatau erupted, causing part of the island to fall into the sea and a tsunami, 2 metres (6.6 feet) high, which killed at least 430 people.

20 PLACES THAT ARE DISAPPEARING

1. The year 2014 was the International Year of Small Island Developing States. It marked the first time the UN had dedicated a year to a specific group of countries to highlight the danger of Indian Ocean islands like the Seychelles being wiped out by the death of corals, which results in beach erosion and the steadily rising sea levels.

2. In 2009, scientists predicted the complete disappearance of the ice cap on Tanzania's Mount Kilimanjaro by 2030.

3. At the 2009 UN Climate Change Conference in Copenhagen, the disappearing Polynesian island nation of Tuvalu submitted a proposed protocol to have binding emission cuts imposed on developing nations.

4. A 2010 study by the Guatemalan Foundation for the Environment found the Maya Biosphere, in Guatemala, which includes the Mirador Basin and Tikal National Park, has lost 64 per cent of its forest in the century's first decade.

5. The Sundarbans in the Ganges Delta, South Asia, are home to the world's largest area of mangrove forests, but a 2013 study by the Zoological Society of London found that the coastline was retreating at about 200 metres (650 feet) a year.

6. A 2012 study by UK scientists showed that since the end of the last Little Ice Age (in 1870) the glaciers of Patagonia, Argentina, have been shrinking continuously. The annual rates of shrinkage though were twice as rapid from 2001 to 2011 as from 1870 to 1986 – most likely due to less rain and snowfall and increased global temperatures. The melting of glacier ice contributed to rising sea levels.

7. The Italian city of Venice has been sinking for a long time, but reports in 2012 suggest that the rate of sinking has now reached 1–2 millimetres each year. With the Adriatic sea rising at the same time, this means that Venice could sink up to 80 millimetres (3.1 inches) by 2032.

8. Natural landslides and an increase in visitor numbers to Peru's famous Inca ruins at Machu Picchu are causing erosion. In 2012, the annual number of visitors surpassed one million for the first time.

9. Between 2007 and 2010 the Galapagos Islands off the coast of Ecuador were put on the UN's World Heritage Danger List due to a growing human presence threatening the unique ecosystem.

10. In 2008, key donor institutions made pledges of $216 million to help save Central Africa's Congo River Basin, two-thirds of which the UN predicted may be completely gone by 2040 without intervention.

11. The water level of the Dead Sea, which borders Jordan and Israel, has dropped by over 40 metres (130 feet) since 1950. The water is evaporating at a rate of over 1 metre (3.3 feet) each year leaving over 3,000 dangerous sinkholes on the new beaches.

12. In 2005, it was announced that one of the world's biggest mining companies would open for business on Madagascar – yet mass deforestation is expected to destroy the island's forests in the next 35 years.

13. In 2018, researchers found that Florida's (USA) mangroves face being drowned by sea-level rises within 30 years, causing a devastating impact to coastal communities and the Everglades wetlands.

14. In 2011, campaigners warned that the iconic Taj Mahal, Agra, India, could collapse within five years because of erosion and rotting foundations – although as of 2019 it remains intact.

15. In 2016, leading scientists warned that, due to rising sea temperatures in the past three decades and acid pollution, Australia's Great Barrier Reef could be completely gone by 2030.

16. Research published in *Science Advances* in 2018 predicted that due to sea-level rises, thousands of islands, including the Marshall Islands (Oceania) and the Maldives (South Asia) will be uninhabitable by the middle of the century.

17. In the late nineteenth century, the Glacier National Park, Montana, USA, was home to over 150 glaciers. Only 26 of them survived up to now, but scientists predicted in 2017 that they too will disappear over the next few decades.

18. Komodo Island, Indonesia, is famed for its endangered Komodo dragons, but tourism and coral bleaching mean the spectacular reefs and wildlife are now under threat.

19. In 2014, Bolivia's second largest body of water, at 2,400 square kilometres (927 square miles), Lake Poopó, faced an unprecedented drought. By late 2015 the lake had dried up completely.

20. In 2015, fears were raised after the *Beijing Times* reported 2,000 kilometres (1,243 miles), or 30 per cent, of the Great Wall of China had disappeared due to human damage and natural erosion.

20 DESTRUCTIVE NATURAL DISASTERS

1. A rock/ice slide in northern Georgia in 2002 occurred after a partial collapse of the Kolka Glacier. The avalanche and mudflow that followed killed 125 people.

2. In 2003, the drought experienced in southern Australia since the late 1990s was officially the worst on record. Often referred to as the 'Millennium Drought', it lasted until 2010.

3. Following an earthquake off Sumatra in the Indian Ocean, a series of large 30 metre (98 foot) high tsunami waves affected over 14 countries on Boxing Day 2004. An estimated 227,898 people were killed. The disaster prompted a global humanitarian response.

4. In 2005, over 1,800 people lost their lives when Hurricane Katrina struck south-east America. The damage amounted to around $125 billion, much of it in New Orleans, making it the costliest hurricane in US history.

5. In 2005, Hurricane Wilma was the Atlantic Basin's most intense tropical cyclone ever recorded. After Wilma made landfall in Florida, USA, it would be 11 years until another hurricane made landfall in the United States.

6. In 2008, Cyclone Nargis became one of the deadliest cyclones in Asia since 1991, causing an estimated 140,000 deaths in India, Thailand, Myanmar, Sri Lanka, Laos and Bangladesh among other countries.

7. Between July and August of 2010 more than 1,700 people were killed when heavy monsoon rains flooded 160,000 square kilometres (61,776 square miles) of north-west Pakistan – almost a fifth of the country.

8. Three million people were affected by the 2010 earthquake and aftershocks in Haiti, the Caribbean, with a shocking death toll put between 100,000 and 160,000 people, although the Haitian government estimated the figure was closer to 300,000.

9. In 2011, the world's fourth most powerful earthquake since records began occurred off the coast of Japan, triggering tsunami waves up to 40.5 metres (133 feet) high, causing nuclear accidents at the Fukushima Daiichi Nuclear Power Plant and killing 15,896 people.

⑩ A severe drought in 2011 affecting the entire East African region led to a famine in Somalia and also affected neighbouring countries. Aid was slow to arrive and approximately 260,000 Somalian people lost their lives.

⑪ An earthquake that struck just 10 kilometres (6.2 miles) south of Christchurch in New Zealand in 2011 killed 185 people and became the deadliest natural disaster in that country this century.

⑫ Hurricane Sandy wreaked havoc during the 2012 Atlantic hurricane season, becoming the second-costliest hurricane on record in the United States and killing 233 people across eight countries.

⑬ One of the strongest tropical cyclones ever recorded was 2013's Typhoon Haiyan, which decimated parts of Southeast Asia, particularly the Philippines where at least 6,300 people died.

⑭ After Hurricane Manuel made landfall twice in September 2013, 107 of Mexico's 2,448 municipalities were declared disaster regions. In the state of Sinaloa alone 100,000 people became homeless as a result.

⑮ An ice avalanche on Mount Everest, the Himalayas, Nepal, made the news in 2014 when 16 climbing Sherpas lost their lives. Only 13 of the bodies were recovered.

⑯ No one died as a result of the 2014 drought in Spain, but as the worst drought in over 150 years, it had a damaging impact on Spain's water reservoirs.

⑰ Heavy snowstorms in Afghanistan's Panjshir Province in 2015 caused 40 avalanches in the region, killing at least 310 people in the country's deadliest avalanches in 30 years.

⑱ 'Hurricane Irma' was the top Google search term of 2017, the year the category-five hurricane caused loss of life and $65 billion worth of damage in the north-eastern Caribbean and Florida Keys, USA.

⑲ When Hurricane Harvey made landfall in the United States in 2017, it joined Katrina at the top of the list of the costliest tropical cyclones on record, with resulting floods displacing more than 30,000 people.

⑳ In January 2017, a luxury hotel resort was struck by an avalanche on one of the mountains above Rigopiano, Italy. It was the deadliest avalanche in Italy for a century and killed 29 people.

20 VERY WET and VERY DRY places

1. Between 24 and 26 of February 2007, Commerson, on the Indian Ocean island of Réunion, recorded its maximum rainfall in a 72-hour period: 3,929 millimetres (155 inches).

2. Then, a day later, it broke the record for the most rainfall in a four-day period, too, with 4,869 millimetres (192 inches).

3. The most snow ever recorded in a 24-hour period fell on Capracotta, Italy, on 5 March 2015. There were 2.56 metres (100 inches) of the white stuff.

4. The most rainfall in the United Kingdom over a 24-hour period occurred in Thirlmere, Cumbria, where it rained 405 millimetres (16 inches) on 5–6 December 2015.

5. Cumbria was also home to new 72-hour and 96-hour rainfall records when between 16 and 19 November in 2009 it rained 456.4 millimetres (18 inches) over three days and 495 millimetres (20 inches) over four days in Seathwaite.

6. But it was Crib Goch in the Snowdonia National Park in Wales that received the highest monthly total rainfall in Britain with a staggering 1,396.4 millimetres (55 inches), a record set in December 2015.

7. In the summer of 2018, Brooms Barn in Suffolk, UK, went 52 consecutive days *without* rainfall, the most rain-free days since 1976. The record from 1893 still stands though: 73 days in East London.

8. One of the wettest major European cities is Podgorica in Montenegro, where on average 1,661 millimetres (65 inches) of rain a year fall on the city.

9. In 2018, a small Hawaiian town broke the all-time US record for rainfall in a 24-hour period: 1,262 millimetres (50 inches) of rain fell on Hanalei, Kauai.

10. And Big Bog, a spot in Haleakala National Park on Maui, Hawaii, USA, climbed into the top ten wettest places on Earth, when between 1978 and 2007 it experienced an average annual rainfall of 10,300 millimetres (404 inches).

11. In recent years, the town of Mawsynram in the East Khasi Hills district of north-eastern India has been considered the wettest place on Earth, with an average annual rainfall of 11,872 millimetres (467 inches).

12. It's usually in stiff competition with its neighbour, Cherrapunjee. Just 15 kilometres (9.3 miles) away, this city's average annual rainfall is 11,777 millimetres (464 inches).

13. Germany's Geysir Andernach holds the record for blowing water higher than any other cold-water geyser – one ejection reached a height of 61.5 metres (202 feet).

14. In 2017, Las Vegas, Nevada, in the USA, broke a 73-year-old record for the region for the number of consecutive days without rain when there were 102 rainless days. The 101-day record was set in 1944.

15. The Atacama Desert in Chile is the driest non-polar desert on Earth, with some areas not receiving rain for 500 years. Although, in 2015, the area received the heaviest rainfall for two decades.

16. In 2017, Yuma in Arizona, USA, was named the sunniest place on Earth, receiving more than 4,000 sunlight hours each year. This puts it ahead of its neighbour Phoenix (3,872 hours) and Aswan, Egypt (3,863 hours).

17. The driest point in Africa is Kufra in Libya. A cultivation project using an underground aquifer aimed to develop agriculture in the desert, but by 2011 exploitation meant the desert lake had completely dried up.

18. Aswan in Egypt is considered the world's driest city – with rainfall not guaranteed each year. When the heavens opened there in 2001, it had been seven years since the last rainy day.

19. According to World Bank data from 1962 and 2014, Colombia remains the wettest country on Earth with an annual rainfall of 3,420 millimetres (128 inches).

20. In the same listing, Egypt is declared the driest country, receiving only 51 millimetres (2 inches) of rain each year.

20 WEIRDEST WEATHER PHENOMENA

1. Hailstones falling on Vivian, South Dakota, USA, in July 2010 broke all existing records. They were measured 20 centimetres (8 inches) in diameter…

2. … Although the stones in South Dakota didn't beat the circumference record. In 2003, in Aurora, Nebraska, USA, hailstones with a circumference of 47.6 centimetres (18.8 inches) were measured.

3. In 2012, hailstones measuring up to 10.2 centimetres (4 inches) in diameter were dropped on the island of Oahu, Hawaii, USA, shattering the state record of 2.5 centimetres (1 inch).

4. The longest lightning bolt in history was recorded in June 2007 in Oklahoma, USA. It measured a staggering 321 kilometres (199 miles).

5. But if you'd been looking up at the sky in Provence, France, on 30 August 2012, you would have witnessed a single lightning flash that lasted for a record 7.74 seconds.

6. Even though Greenland is mostly known for its icy landscape, in summer 2017 satellites detected a series of wildfires.

7. Red rain, coloured by a prolific local alga, fell on Kerala, India, between July and September 2001. The phenomenon is known as blood rain.

8. But that was nothing compared to the 'animal rains' reported throughout history, including 3,000 blackbirds falling from the sky in Beebe, Arkansas, USA, in December 2010 – their deaths believed to be caused by fireworks.

9. Fish rained down in Wales in 2004, Australia in 2010 and Mexico in 2017, among other places. It's thought that these animal rains might be caused by tornadic waterspouts picking up animals and then dumping them, sometimes miles away.

10. It was the turn of the tadpole to fall from the sky in Japan's Ishikawa Prefecture over two days in June 2009. Residents in Nanao and Hakusan reported the phenomenon.

11. Ball lightning has been recorded since the seventeenth century but was only caught on camera for the first time in 2012 by Chinese researchers in Qinghai.

12. Between January and March 2010, the unique Catatumbo lightning phenomenon observed at the mouth of the Catatumbo River in South America ceased because of a drought. It normally occurs 260 nights a year.

13. In late 2013, tourists at the Grand Canyon, Arizona, USA, witnessed a rare weather phenomenon, where fog filled the entire canyon, appearing like a cloud waterfall. It only happens around once every decade.

14. A rare 'super derecho' storm, made up of multiple thunderstorms and strong winds, left a path of destruction in its wake when it travelled across the American Midwest and mid-Atlantic in June 2012.

15. In 2018, the Carr Fire, which destroyed nearly 230,000 acres (93,000 hectares) in California, USA, also created a fire vortex on 26 July that year – a blazing funnel of fire with winds reaching 143 mph (230 kph).

16. In 2018, a new study revealed how volcanic lightning can be used as a monitoring tool to track the dangers of a volcanic eruption.

17. The streets of Stravropol, Russia, were coated with multicoloured snow in 2010. The purple and brown snow was thought to be contaminated by dust that travelled from Africa.

18. A year later, residents on America's east coast witnessed lightning and thunder during a snow storm, a phenomenon known as 'thundersnow'.

19. While tornadoes are common, twin tornadoes, like the ones seen in Pilger, Nebraska, USA, in 2014, are extremely rare, only occurring every 10 to 20 years.

20. Tsunamis do not only happen on Earth. Two satellites spotted a tsunami on the surface of the sun. It helped scientists to understand the dynamics of these devastating Earthly events.

20 HIGHEST AND LOWEST TEMPERATURES

❶ The second-highest temperature recorded in history in Africa was in July 2018. Ouargla in Algeria recorded 51.3°C (124.3°F). The record still belongs to El Azizia, Libya where 57.8°C (136°F) was measured on 13 September 1922.

❷ 2015 was the year Antarctica recorded its second-highest temperature on record since 1982 – 17.5°C (63.5°F) – at Esperanza Base, Trinity Peninsula.

❸ In 2017, Ahwaz Airport in Iran equalled the highest temperature ever recorded in Asia. Temperatures soared to 54°C (129°F), the same as Tirat Zvi, Israel, in 1942.

❹ The Greece-held European record from 1977, 48°C (118.4°F), has yet to be beaten, but in 2003, Portugal came close when Amareleja in Beja reached 47.4°C (117.3°F).

❺ And, more recently, summer visitors to Montoro, Spain, sweltered in the July 2017 heat – it was a 47.3°C (117.1°F).

❻ Records for North America have not been broken since 1913, when temperatures soared to 56.7°C (134°F) at Furnace Creek, California.

❼ Records were also set in the British Virgin Islands and the Cayman Islands, in the Caribbean, a year later when both places recorded their highest ever temperatures: 35°C (95°F) and 34.9°C (94.8°F) respectively.

❽ But Death Valley, California, USA, took the world record for the highest average monthly temperature in 2018 when, for the month of July, it averaged 42.3°C (108.1°F).

❾ Needles in California, USA, also earned a record for having the highest temperature during rainfall, when it was 46.1°C (115.0°F) during a downpour in 2012.

10. The northerly Yukon territory in Canada recorded its highest temperature on record in June 2004 – 36.5°C (97.7°F).

11. Oodnadatta, Australia still holds the record for the hottest place in Oceania, when it reached 50.7°C (123.3°F) in 1960, but in 2016 the Pacific Island of Vanuatu became the third hottest with 36.2°C (97.2°F).

12. In South America, Villamontes, Bolivia, got up to 46.7°C (116.1°F) in 2010, making it the second hottest place on the continent.

13. It might have been home to the second hottest spot in Africa, but Mécheria, Algeria, was also one of the continent's coldest spots. In 2005, it got down to –13.8°C (7.2°F).

14. It was colder again in South Africa, however, where in Eastern Cape it reached –20.1°C (–4.2°F) in 2013.

15. Records from the 1980s still stand in Antarctica, but in 2005, Dome Argus – the Antarctic Plateau's loftiest ice dome – was a shivering –82.5°C (–116.5°F), the third coldest temperature recorded.

16. Siberia is on record as the coldest place in Asia, with historical records from February 1933 showing temperatures as low as –67.8°C (–90°F). This record was only just missed, when in 2018 temperatures sank to –67°C (–88°F) in Oymyakon, which is considered the world's coldest permanently inhabited town.

17. Pale di San Martino in Italy became the fifth coldest recorded place in Europe in 2013. It was –49.6°C (–57.2°F) in the mountain range.

18. Chile's Coyhaique Alto recorded the lowest ever temperatures in South America in 2002. It was –37°C (–34.6°F).

19. Greenland, Canada and the USA have all recorded temperatures in the region of –60°C (–76°F) in the past, but, so far, nothing in the twenty-first century has come close. In 2009 and 2011, respectively, Maine and Oklahoma in the USA recorded record state lows of –50°C (–58°F) and –31°C (–29°F).

20. Summit Camp, Greenland, recorded the coldest summer in July 2017 with average temperatures of –33°C (–27.4°F).

20 FEROCIOUS WILDFIRES

1. In July 2000, parts of southern France, Italy, Iberia and Corsica were consumed by wildfires, which were exacerbated by the summer heatwave when temperatures soared to 45°C (113°F).

2. The Siberian forest fires of 2003 had 19 million hectares (7 million acres) of land in flames and is considered the largest so far. The effect of these fires can still be seen in studies on ozone depletion.

3. Sixty different fire departments tried to control the 2003 firestorm in Okanagan Mountain Provincial Park in British Columbia, Canada. About 27,000 residents had to be evacuated.

4. That same year in California, USA, the state recorded the third largest fire in modern history when 2,232 homes were destroyed and 15 people killed in the Cedar Fire in San Diego County.

5. A series of wildfires in autumn 2007 covered over 800,000 hectares (2 million acres) and burned 1,500 homes from Santa Barbara, California, USA, to the Mexican border.

6. While in Croatia the coast was struck by around 750 fires in the summer of 2007. Police later indicted 18 people for arson.

7. The Black Saturday bushfires burned across Victoria, Australia, on 7 February 2009. They were among the country's worst ever bushfires with the most fatalities: 180.

8. Wildfires raged in the Mediterranean in July 2009, with France, Spain, Turkey, Greece and Italy all affected. Some of the fires were caused by lightning and illegal scrub burning.

9. A state of emergency was declared in Bolivia in 2010 when more than 25,000 fires, covering nearly 1.6 million hectares (4 million acres), burned across the country, particularly in the Amazon region.

10. Israel's most deadly forest fire was the Mount Carmel blaze of 2010. The fast-spreading fire claimed 44 lives and 17,000 people had to be evacuated.
11. On 30 June 2013, 19 firefighters lost their lives – the most firefighters killed in a fire since 1933 – during the Yarnell Hill Fire in Arizona, USA.
12. The Great Fire of Valparaíso in Chile started in April 2014, destroying 2,500 homes and destroying the communities of 11,000 people.
13. In 2015, a forest fire that burned through just under 52,000 hectares (128,500 acres) in Indonesia was considered too dangerous for human intervention. The haze drifted to Malaysia, Thailand, Vietnam and the Philippines.
14. In 2016, the Fort McMurray wildfire 600,000 hectares (1.5 million acres) in Alberta, Canada, made international news. With estimated damages of C$9.9 billion, it was Canada's costliest natural disaster on record and required over 90,000 people to be evacuated.
15. More than 100 people were trapped and killed by two separate series of wildfires in Portugal in June and October 2017.
16. Another notable Californian wildfire also took place in October 2017. The series of fires spanned 97,000 hectares (240,000 acres) and claimed 44 lives.
17. Meanwhile, also in 2017, residents in Christchurch, New Zealand, looked on as the nearby Port Hills caught fire. The only fatality was caused when a helicopter that was helping to fight the fires crashed, killing the pilot.
18. A record-breaking series of wildfires, engulfing 3,600 hectares (9,000 acres), started burning on Saddleworth Moor in the north of England in June 2018. They were exacerbated by a heatwave reaching above 30°C (86°F) for several days.
19. Greece faced far worse devastation the following month when 100 people were confirmed dead after the world's second-deadliest wildfires of the twenty-first century.
20. The third-deadliest occurred a few months later when Camp Fire ravaged Northern California, USA. From November 2018 the fire took 17 days to contain and killed 83 people.

Flora and Fauna

20 AMAZING ANIMALS

1. Around a hundred search and rescue and cadaver dogs worked at the Ground Zero site after 9/11. One guide dog, Roselle, led her blind owner from the 78th storey of the North Tower to the safety of a subway station.
2. It was 2002 when Australian farmer Noel Osborne broke his hip and was stranded for five days with just Mandy the goat for company. She kept him warm and let him drink her milk.
3. Yang Yun owes her life to a beluga whale at Polar Land in Harbin, China. She had been taking part in a free diving contest in which competitors had to swim to the bottom of an arctic pool, which was 6 metres (20 feet) deep, and stay there for as long as possible. The large tank was also home to beluga whales, one of which spotted diver Yang Yun struggling as her legs paralysed with crippling cramps due to the cold temperatures, and helped her to the surface.
4. Quaker parrot Willie came to the rescue in 2009 when it alerted its owner that the toddler she was babysitting was choking on a Pop Tart. He squawked repeatedly and said 'mama baby'.
5. Grumpy Cat, whose real name is Tardar Sauce, became a movie star when she starred in 2014's *Grumpy Cat's Worst Christmas Ever*.
6. Irene Ahn's adorable Pomeranian dog Boo became the furry face of Virgin America in 2012. Boo is worth over $8 million.
7. And Boo's not the only star making millions – Taylor Swift's cat Olivia Benson has a booming online following and has made herself a reported $97 million for starring in ads for Coke and Keds Shoes in 2018.
8. In 2000, Bart the Bear, an Alaskan Kodiak bear who starred in over 20 films, including *Legends of the Fall* and *White Fang*, passed away. He was trained by Doug Seus, who is now caring for Bart the Bear II, star of *Game of Thrones* and *Into the Wild*.
9. In 2007, 24-year-old Todd Endris was surfing in the waters off Monterey Bay, California, USA, when he was attacked by a shark. A school of dolphins came to his rescue and surrounded him, creating a wall between him and the shark.

10. In 2015, loggers on Vangunu, in the Solomon Islands, felled a tree to discover a giant new species of rat. Weighing more than 900 grams (2 pounds) and growing up to 46 centimetres (1.5 feet) long, it gave them quite a fright.

11. In 2003, Keiko, the killer whale that starred in the film *Free Willy,* died a year after his real-life release into the wild. He died of pneumonia after a five-year-long battle to return him to his natural habitat.

12. In 2010, a duck was hit by a van in Belgium – but survived not only the crash, but also the following immensely long journey to West Yorkshire, UK, where it emerged from under the bonnet.

13. In 2013, the deep sea blobfish beat the proboscis monkey and axolotl to be chosen by the public as the new mascot of the Ugly Animal Preservation Society.

14. In 2005, three lions rescued a 12-year-old girl who had been kidnapped and held for a week by men in Ethiopia. The lions stood guard until police and her family found her.

15. When the 2004 Indian Ocean tsunami struck Thailand, a British girl was riding Ningnong, an elephant, who ran to higher ground, protecting her from the worst of the wave.

16. A penguin at Edinburgh Zoo in Scotland, named Colonel-in-Chief Nils Olav II, was honoured with a knighthood by Norway's King's Guard in 2008. Nils Olav III, the penguin's son, was made a Brigadier in 2016.

17. A rare white giraffe calf, whose skin cells don't produce pigmentation, was spotted in Tanzania's Tarangire National Park in 2016. She was named Omo after a popular local brand of laundry detergent.

18. In 2017, an American badger in Utah's Great Basin excavated tunnels beneath a calf carcass until the whole thing collapsed into a pit. The badger proceeded to bury the calf and eat it for 11 days – the largest badger entombing recorded.

19. In 2004, a diabetic British man fell unconscious while watching television. His pet rabbit, Dory, jumped onto his chest and started thumping furiously, alerting his wife's attention.

20. Robert Biggs was hiking in north-central California, USA, in 2012 and admiring a bear and her cub when he was attacked by a mountain lion. Luckily the mother bear came to his rescue, pouncing on the lion and scaring it off.

20 Valuable Crops and Livestock

1. The world's most valuable crop is paddy rice. In 2012, the world produced $337 billion worth of rice; China was 2016's biggest producer, with a value of $117 billion.

2. In terms of livestock, cattle come top with a 2012 valuation of $336 billion. The United States was the world's largest cattle producer in 2016.

3. Unsurprisingly, the United States is also the world's biggest producer of cow's milk, the world's second most valuable livestock product. In 2016 milk was a $35 billion industry.

4. Wheat is frequently the second most valuable crop. In 2014, the cereal was grown on more land area than any other crop.

5. Maize or corn is big business, too, particularly in the Americas. In 2011, it was the second most produced crop in terms of volume, with 885 million tonnes (871 million tons).

6. Nigeria is the world's biggest producer of cassava or yuca (a root vegetable). In the tropics it's the third-largest source of carbohydrates after rice and maize.

7. The United States, Brazil and Argentina combined were responsible for 81 per cent of the world's soybean production in 2016.

8. While in 2012, China was the biggest producer of tomatoes. However, the Netherlands' tomato farms were more productive, with a nationwide average of 476 tonnes (468 tons) of tomatoes per hectare.

9. In terms of volume, sugar cane is the world's most produced crop by far, with 1.8 billion tonnes (1.7 billion tons) in 2011 alone.

10. 377 million tonnes (371 million tons) of potatoes were produced in 2016. Major producers are China, India, Russia, Ukraine and the United States.

11. Nearly three-quarters of world grape production is used to make wine, with the rest for fresh and dried fruit. Spain has the most land dedicated to wine grape growing, but China is the biggest grape producer.

12. Egg production was a $54 billion global industry in 2012. In 2013 the four largest producers were China, the United States, India and Japan.

13. The world seems to love apples. In 2014, 84.6 million tonnes (83 million tons) were produced around the world, with nearly half of these being grown in China.

14. In 2016, 29 per cent of the world's bananas were grown in India. But the biggest banana exporters were Ecuador and the Philippines who each shipped 5.4 and 3.3 million tonnes (5.3 and 3.2 tons) of the fruit that year.

15. Cow's milk might be a world leader, but water buffalo milk is a $38 billion global industry, with the biggest producers being India and Pakistan.

16. Mangoes are the fourth most valuable fruit industry. India is the largest producer, contributing 40 per cent of the world's mangoes, with China and Thailand the next largest.

17. In 2009, China and India were the largest cotton producers, most of which is used by their own textile industries. The United States as the third largest producer was the largest exporter.

18. Indonesia is the largest producer of palm oil – an industry valued at $39.3 billion in 2016 – producing 20.9 million tonnes (20.5 million tons) a year. By 2030 that figure is expected to double.

19. In 2016, 44 million tonnes (43 million tons) of peanuts were produced around the world, with huge quantities grown in China and India. India was the largest exporter, shipping 32 per cent of the world's total peanut exports.

20. The United States provides 63 per cent of the world's almonds, with most of them coming from California. In 2017, 405,000 hectares (1 million acres) of the state was dedicated to producing six almond varieties.

20 SPECIES THAT HAVE BECOME ENDANGERED OR EXTINCT

1. While the Pyrenean ibex goat was once a common sight in the Pyrenees, the species was declared extinct in 2000. In 2009, scientists tried using frozen tissue to create clones.

2. In 2008, the Caribbean monk seal, the only seal species native to the region, earned the regrettable title of being the first seal species to be wiped out because of human activity.

3. Western black rhinoceroses were seen for the final time in Cameroon, but substantial hunting throughout the twentieth century saw the population dwindle. In 2011, it was declared extinct.

4. The last known Pinta Island tortoise, a 100-year-old named Lonesome George, died in captivity in 2015. The species was native to the Galapagos Islands but wiped out by goats that humans introduced there.

5. The Formosan clouded leopard was once the second largest carnivorous animal in Taiwan, but logging has eradicated this species and it was declared extinct in 2013.

6. 2011 saw the US Fish and Wildlife Service (USFWS) carry out a review of the eastern cougar, concluding that while the western cougar and Florida panther continue to breed, there was no evidence of the eastern subspecies.

7. Scientists believe temperature rises caused by climate change created ideal conditions for a deadly fungus, *chytridiomycosis*, that had wiped out Costa Rica's golden toad population by 2004.

8. 2004 was a bad year for Costa Rica – the Heredia robber frog was also declared extinct, and scientists think the same fungus, *chytridiomycosis*, might be to blame.

9. Endemic to the Yangtze River in China, the Chinese paddlefish population was severely affected by the 1981 Gezhouba Dam construction. The last recorded sightings were in 2003.

10. Another Yangtze species, the baiji dolphin, became the most threatened cetacean in the world in 2008. No baiji have been spotted since 2002.

11. The Vietnamese Javan rhino became critically endangered in 2008, and the only known surviving female was shot and killed in the Cát Tiên National Park in April 2010.

12. A tiny bat species endemic to Christmas Island, Australia, the pipistrella, is believed to be extinct after the last known one went missing in 2009.

13. Incapable of long-distance flying, the small-winged Alaotra Grebe was a lake-dwelling Madagascan bird species that was relisted as extinct in 2010.

14. In 2006, Israel's Long Jaw fish was critically endangered. Eight years later, it was relisted as extinct. Researchers believe destruction of its breeding habitat in Kinneret Lake could be the reason for extinction.

15. The mountain forests of the Hawaiian island of Maui, USA, were once home to the black-faced honeycreeper or po'o-uli. By the 1970s there were only 200 of the birds left in the wild. None have been spotted since 2004.

16. Sumatran orangutans were declared critically endangered in 2008. In 2016, their cousins, the Bornean orangutan, were given the same designation. Populations have declined by 60 per cent since 1950.

17. In 2018, the US Fish and Wildlife Service (USFWS) announced that the wild population of red wolves was down to just 40 animals from 120 in 2013. They predicted that the species would be extinct in the wild within eight years.

18. In 2010, the Zoological Society of London added the scaly anteaters (pangolins), of which there are eight species, to its list of evolutionarily distinct and endangered mammals. It is currently the most trafficked mammal on Earth.

19. South-eastern Russia and north-eastern China are home to the critically endangered Amur leopard. In 2007 there were thought to be less than 26 surviving in the wild.

20. The world's rarest marine animal is a small porpoise called a vaquita. In 2017, the International Committee for the Recovery of the Vaquita reported that there were just 30 left in the Upper Gulf of California, North America – its only known habitat.

20 Popular Dog Breeds

1. According to the American Kennel Club, Labrador Retrievers were the United States's most popular dog breed in 2006, 2007, 2008 and from 2013 to 2018.

2. They were the top dog in the United Kingdom too, although the Cocker Spaniel came in second place for four out of five years in a row between 2013 and 2017, despite not even making the top 20 in the United States.

3. The English Springer is another breed that is consistently well-liked by the British. It's often ranked in the top five (although never in first or second place).

4. Second place five years running in the United States was the German Shepherd – in 2017 it was the United Kingdom's eighth most popular breed with 7,479 puppies registered.

5. In 2018, the French Bulldog overtook the Labrador to become the United Kingdom's most popular dog for the first time. It was in fourth place in the United States that same year.

6. Between 2005 and 2011 the Pug's popularity soared in the United Kingdom by 170 per cent.

7. The Golden Retriever, similar in appearance to its Labrador cousin, was the Americans' third most popular dog between 2013 and 2018.

8. French Bulldogs meant big business too. But despite the growth in their popularity, they hovered around sixth or seventh place through the 2010s in the UK and fourth and fifth in the US.

9. Poodles are a firm favourite of the Canadians – they have regularly been the country's fourth most popular dog breed throughout the last 20 years.

10. Border Collies have been the number one dog three times in Norway, including in 2016.

⓫ Despite the success of other miniature dogs, Miniature Schnauzers sit nearer the bottom of the list in the United States – ranked at number 18 in 2017 – and don't appear in the top 10 in the United Kingdom either. Perhaps it's their grumpy-looking faces?

⓬ Staffordshire Bull Terriers normally rank in the United Kingdom top 20. They were also the most likely dog to end up in rescue centres according to the RSPCA.

⓭ In 2007, the Cavalier King Charles spaniel was still the United Kingdom's sixth most popular breed. But by 2016 its numbers had halved and the breed dropped to thirteenth in the rankings.

⓮ Rottweilers leapt from tenth place in 2014 to eighth place in 2017 in the American Kennel Club's rankings.

⓯ While it's still in the top ten (at number nine in 2018) the Yorkshire Terrier was the United States's second most popular dog breed ten years earlier.

⓰ The German Short-Haired Pointer made the news in 2018 when it broke into the top ten list of most popular dog breeds in the United States.

⓱ In 2017, the Havanese stole the coveted fifth position on the Canadian popular dogs podium from the Shetland Sheepdog, which had held the spot since 2005.

⓲ Between 2007 and 2016 the number of Smooth-Coat Chihuahuas had nearly trebled in the United Kingdom, from 1,142 to 3,394.

⓳ Dalmatians saw a surge in popularity in the United Kingdom after the 1985 release of *101 Dalmatians* but were no longer in the top 20 there in the 2000s. In Australia, however, they were the ninth most popular dog in 2007.

⓴ In 2018, the most popular breed in Japan was the Miniature Dachshund, making up 13 per cent of all pet dogs.

20 Genetic Modifications

1. Originally developed in the 1990s to improve vitamin A intake in developing countries, 2005 saw Golden Rice get an upgrade, with a new version that produced 23 times more beta-carotene (an antioxidant that in humans converts to vitamin A) than the original.

2. Cotton seeds typically contain a natural bug deterrent called gossypol that makes them inedible. In 2006, Texas A&M University in the USA collaborated with Cotton Inc. to produce edible cotton seeds that could be used to make flour.

3. In 2007, Monsanto's Roundup Ready sugar beets became available to farmers in the USA. Three years later 95 per cent of all beets grown in the United States were of the herbicide-resistant strain.

4. BioCassava Plus received funding from the Bill and Melinda Gates Foundation to develop a virus-resistant version of the root vegetable cassava that contains increased nutrients. Field trials took place in 2007 in Puerto Rico and 2009 in Nigeria.

5. A new onion, which could be chopped without making you cry, was announced in 2008 after tests by New Zealand Crop & Food Research.

6. Researchers at Texas A&M AgriLife's Vegetable and Fruit Improvement Center produced a new carrot in 2008 that could help people absorb more calcium.

7. Biofortified Soya Beans were first approved commercially in 1994. In 2010 DuPont Pioneer started marketing a high oleic fatty acid soya bean to improve oil production.

8. It was the same year that the limited production of 'Enviropigs' was approved by Environment Canada. The genetically modified animals produce urine and faeces that contain 65 per cent less environment-damaging phosphorous.

9. In 2012, field trials were underway for another type of genetically modified rice – this time a flood-resistant version – developed by the International Rice Research Institute in the Philippines...

⑩ … And a biotechnology company genetically modified industrial yeast to make it eat agricultural waste and excrete crude oil.

⑪ In 2013, scientists announced they were working on producing a strain of the flowering plant jatropha that could grow well in arid conditions. The plant's seeds produce a palm-oil-type of liquid that could be used as biofuel.

⑫ The John Innes Centre in Norwich, United Kingdom, developed a purple tomato, which contains the pigment anthocyanin, an antioxidant that could help fight cancer. In 2014, large-scale production of the tomato for testing was underway in Canada.

⑬ Two researchers at the US Department of Agriculture were able to genetically alter a castor bean plant to block the production of the deadly toxin ricin as well as allergens in order to make it safer to grow.

⑭ In 2016, scientists at Israel's Agricultural Research Organization developed banana plants that give the popular fruit a longer shelf life.

⑮ A year later trials were ongoing for a Maris Piper potato created by the Sainsbury Laboratory in Norwich, United Kingdom, that had been modified with blight resistance genes.

⑯ In 2017, the Arctic apple went on sale in the USA. The genetically modified variety resists browning after being cut, protecting its flavour and nutritional value.

⑰ It was the same year that the Canadian authorities allowed salmon, genetically modified by AquaBounty, to reach market size in half the usual growing time, to be sold to consumers.

⑱ In 2018, scientists were working on a genetically modified groundcherry (physalis) to make the Central and South American fruit easier to grow commercially.

⑲ Also in 2018, *The Guardian* reported that Scotland's Roslin Institute was working to genetically modify chickens to give them an extra avian-flu gene, helping to interrupt the transmission of the virus.

⑳ The Roslin Institute also announced that year that they had deleted the section of pig DNA that leaves the animal vulnerable to porcine reproductive and respiratory syndrome.

20 Record-Breaking Fruits and Veggies

1. In 2001, the biggest bunch of bananas recorded contained 473 individual bananas and was grown at the Finca Experimental de las Calmas on El Hierro, Canary Islands.

2. Japanese grower Manabu Oono became a record holder in 2003 with his giant radish, weighing in at 31.1 kilograms (68 pounds 9 ounces), which he presented at the Sakurajima Radish Contest.

3. One specimen of Mammoth Purple Top Turnip transformed into the world record holder in 2004. It weighed 17.7 kilograms (39 pounds 3 ounces) and was grown by Americans Scott and Mardie Robb.

4. In 2016, Joe Atherton broke his own 2007 record for the world's longest carrot. In 2016, at the UK National Giant Vegetables Championship, his carrot was 6.245 metres (over 20 feet) long.

5. The record for the world's heaviest carrot is currently held by Christopher Qualley from Minnesota, USA. His 2017 beast weighed in at 10.17 kilograms (22 pounds 7 ounces).

6. The heaviest cabbage, according to Guinness World Records, was presented at the Alaska State Fair, USA, in 2012. It was grown by Alaskan Scott Robb (the world record holder for the heaviest turnip) and weighed 62.71 kilograms (138 pounds 4 ounces).

7. In 2016, Mathias Willemijns from Belgium broke the world record for growing the heaviest pumpkin. It weighed 1,190 kilograms (2,624 pounds).

8. The heaviest tomato on the other hand, was light by comparison – Dan Sutherland's record-breaking tomato was weighed in at 3.906 kilograms (8 pounds 9 ounces) in Washington, USA, in 2016.

9. The heaviest pomelo, a large citrus fruit, was a Japanese variety called Banpeiyu grown by a school in Yatsushiro, Japan. It officially broke the record in 2014 with a weight of 4.86 kilograms (10 pounds 11 ounces) and a diameter of 28.1 centimetres (11.1 inches).

10. However, the largest orange by circumference measured 63.5 centimetres (25 inches) around its widest point in 2006. It belonged to Patrick and Joanne Fiedler of Fresno, California.

11. Felicidad Pasalo, who lives in Hawaii, USA, broke the world record for the heaviest avocado in 2018. The fruit, which is native to Hawaii, weighed in at 2.495 kilograms (5 pounds 8 ounces).

12. That was also the year Agricola Santa Azul in Lima, Peru, broke the record for the heaviest blueberry. The Eureka variety berry weighed 15 grams (0.5 ounces) and had a diameter of 3.45 centimetres (1.4 inches).

13. The heaviest potato record was broken in 2011 when Peter Glazebrook showed off his bounty at the National Gardening Show in Somerset, UK. It weighed 4.98 kilograms (10 pounds 14 ounces).

14. But by comparison, the heaviest sweet potato dwarfs it. The 2004 record still stands: the giant root vegetable, grown by Manuel Pérez Pérez in Lanzarote, tipped the scales at 37 kilograms (81 pounds 9 ounces).

15. In 2014, the world's largest truffle, weighing 1.8 kilograms (63 ounces), which was found in central Italy, was sold to a Chinese phone bidder by Sotheby's auction house for $61,250.

16. Dutch vegetable grower Bradley Wursten presented the world's largest marrow in 2009 at the Dutch Giant Vegetable Championship. It weighed 93.7 kilograms (206 pounds 8 ounces).

17. The heaviest beetroot record has been held since 2001 when British grower Ian Neale claimed the title: the beetroot weighed 23.4 kilograms (nearly 52 pounds).

18. In 2014, Japan's Hokuto Corporation managed to grow the world's longest edible mushroom, *Pleurotus eryngii*, – at 59 centimetres (23 inches).

19. Another Japanese record occurred a year later when Chisato Iwasaki's apple farm in Hirosaki City produced the world's heaviest apple. It weighed nearly 2 kilograms (4 pounds 7 ounces).

20. The world's hottest chilli pepper was a Carolina Reaper, grown by Ed Currie at the PuckerButt Pepper Company. It rated an average of 1.64 million Scoville Heat Units in 2017.

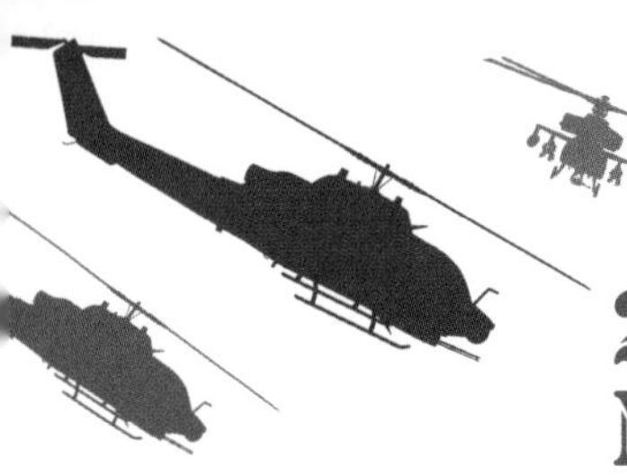

20 MOST NOTABLE CONFLICTS

1. The deadliest war of the twenty-first century so far, the Second Congo War (1998–2003), saw an estimated three million people, mostly civilians, die in the fighting or from disease and malnutrition.

2. After the 9/11 terror attacks in 2001, the US-led 'War on Terror' focused on the Taliban regime in Afghanistan. The resulting conflict led to the deaths of 3,500 coalition forces and 31,000 Afghan civilians.

3. The systematic massacre of some 300,000 civilians in Darfur, Sudan, by the government-supported Arab militia group Janjaweed was described by the US government as the first genocide of the twenty-first century.

4. The Iraq War (2003–2011), led by the United States and a 'coalition of the willing', toppled Saddam Hussein's Ba'athist regime and led to a long insurgency, 4,700 coalition deaths and over 85,000 dead Iraqis.

5. The Arab Spring uprising in Syria (2011–2012) became a civil war that spread into neighbouring Iraq, causing four million people to be displaced, and became a breeding ground for militant groups, such as ISIS.

6. The war against Islamist militant group Boko Haram in Nigeria began after a series of terrorist raids in 2009. Nigerian government forces hit back hard, and a full-blown insurgency followed.

7. The Yemeni Civil War (2015–present), born out of the Arab Spring, resulted in an assassination attempt on President ʿAlī ʿAbd Allāh Ṣāliḥ and international involvement from a Saudi Arabia-led coalition.

8. From 2013, the conflict in Ukraine saw some 10,000 people killed, mostly civilians, the annexation of Crimea, and the shooting down of Malaysia Airlines flight MH17 by pro-Russian forces.

9. From 2006, the Mexican government has been at war with the drug trafficking syndicates and they with each other. Since then, cartel warfare has led to some 150,000 homicides.

10. The Second Chechen War resulted in a nine-year-long insurgency, from the year 2000, between the Chechen Republic of Ichkeria and the Russian Federation.

11. In February 2009, conflict between the government and African Union peacekeeping forces, as well as various terrorist groups, erupted, displacing thousands of people. The conflict is ongoing.

12. The Libyan Civil War of 2011 lasted eight months, and saw rebel forces overthrow the Libyan Arab Jamahiriya system of leader Muammar Gaddafi, who was also killed in the conflict.

13. Violence intensified in the Israeli–Palestinian conflict between 2000 and 2005 in a period known as the Second Intifada...

14. ... From 2005 onwards, the conflict continued, notably with the 2006 Lebanon War and the Battle of Gaza...

15. ... From 2015–2016 there was a further wave of violence across the region with nearly 300 deaths, and thousands injured.

16. The ongoing civil conflict in Myanmar erupted in 2016 with clashes between Burmese security forces and the insurgent group Harakah al-Yaqin, later known as the Arakan Rohingya Salvation Army.

17. An insurgency led by the nomadic Tuareg of northern Mali and Islamist rebels gathered momentum in 2007, and there was a military coup in 2012. In 2013, France sent in troops and launched air strikes.

18. Regarded as the first European war of the twenty-first century, a five-day conflict took place in August 2008 between Russia and Georgia in the strategically important Transcaucasia region.

19. The Philippine government's war on drugs began in 2016 when President Rodrigo Duterte urged the public to kill suspected criminals and drug addicts. The death tolls vary, but some estimates say between 12,000 and 20,000 have died as a result.

20. The Sinai insurgency is an ongoing conflict in Egypt's Sinai Peninsular between Egyptian security forces and Islamist militants. It started in the wake of the Egyptian revolution in 2011.

20 RELIGIONS OF THE TWENTY-FIRST CENTURY

1. A 2010 Pew Research Center study found that 31 per cent of the world's population (2.17 billion people) are Christian.

2. Fifty per cent of these are Catholic. According to the Vatican in 2017, the continent with the fastest-growing Catholic population is Africa.

3. Thirty-seven per cent are classified as Protestant, meaning they belong to one of many denominations, including Baptist churches, Lutheranism, Methodism and Presbyterianism.

4. Twelve per cent are members of the Eastern Orthodox Church – 2010 research showed that 14 per cent of the world's Eastern Orthodox population live in Ethiopia.

5. One per cent of the world's Christians come from another Christian denomination, such as Mormonism or Jehovah's Witnesses.

6. Twenty-three per cent of the world's population (1.6 billion people) are Muslim. In 2017, Pew Research predicted that Islam is likely to surpass Christianity as the world's largest religious group in the second half of the twenty-first century.

7. Eighty-seven to ninety per cent of those are Sunnis. The countries with the largest Sunni majorities are Egypt, Indonesia, Bangladesh and Pakistan.

8. And 10–13 per cent are Shia. There are only four countries that have a Shia majority: Iran, Azerbaijan, Bahrain and Iraq.

9. The next largest religious group is Hinduism with 15 per cent of the world's population, or just over one billion people – 94 per cent of Hindus live in India.

10. There are 488 million Buddhists, half of whom live in China. The percentage of the world's population that is Buddhist is expected to decline by 2050 because of low fertility rates in Buddhist cultures.

11. There are 405 million people who belong to faiths closely associated with a particular group, ethnicity or tribe – these are referred to as 'folk religions'.

12. About 0.2 per cent of the world's population, 13.9 million people, are Jewish. The majority of these live in the United States (41 per cent) or Israel (41 per cent).

13. Around 1 per cent of the world's population belong to a number of other religions. People who identified as having no religion made up about 16 per cent of the population in 2015.

14. There are approximately 25 million Sikhs. The largest population of Sikhs, over 20 million, can be found in the Punjab region of India.

15. There are 20 million members of the Taoist faith. Taoism (or Daoism) has seen a resurgence in China in recent years.

16. Five to six million people are members of the Baha'i faith, and there are a similar number of Confucianists.

17. Four million people are Jainists, and a similar number follow the Shinto faith. Shinto is the dominant religion in Japan, with 80 per cent of the population practising, although most don't identify with any organised religious group.

18. There are believed to be one million to three million Wiccans – Wicca is a pagan religion, typically worshipping a goddess and a god, with its origins in pre-Christian traditions.

19. The controversial, celebrity-endorsed Scientology is thought to have around 100,000–500,000 followers, although some have suggested the numbers might be closer to 20,000.

20. And in some countries, people identify as Jedi, the religious order from the Star Wars universe. In 2011, there were nearly 177,000 Jedis on the UK national census.

20 cyber attacks

❶ In 2010, Albert Gonzalez was sentenced to 20 years in federal prison for masterminding the theft of 134 million credit cards, which were exposed through credit card processor Heartland's data systems.

❷ Gonzalez was also behind a 2006 breach of TJX (the company that owns TJ Maxx and Marshalls). He was working as an informant for the US Secret Service at the time, but that didn't stop him leading a gang who stole 94 million credit cards.

❸ In 2010, an attack targeting Siemens SCADA systems damaged Iran's nuclear programme, destroying hundreds of uranium enrichment centrifuges – the attack was attributed to the United States and Israel, but there's been no official acknowledgement.

❹ Sony's PlayStation Network was down for a month in 2011 after hacking led to 77 million accounts affected – the company then faced a class action lawsuit from disgruntled customers.

❺ *Sesame Street*'s YouTube channel was hacked in 2011. The hackers were able to stream 22 minutes of pornographic content.

❻ Social networking website LinkedIn was hacked in 2012, with the user passwords for nearly 6.5 million of its accounts stolen.

❼ User records for 38 million Adobe customers were hacked in 2013. The company had to pay customers $1.1 million in damages.

❽ In 2013 and 2014, Yahoo user accounts were the target of two data breaches. Yahoo later estimated that some three billion accounts had been compromised.

❾ According to a *New York Times* report, the 2014–2018 hack on the hotel chain Marriott International, where cyber thieves stole the data of 500 million customers, was carried out by a Chinese intelligence group, wanting to gather data on American citizens.

10. 2014 was the year 76 million households (more than half of the United States) and 7 million small businesses were victims of the JP Morgan Chase data breach.

11. Hacker group Guardians of Peace held Sony Pictures Entertainment to ransom in 2014 when they demanded Sony withdraw their film *The Interview* from release. They published confidential data, including personal information and emails between employees.

12. In 2015, Ashley Madison, a website that enables extramarital affairs, was hacked. The hackers threatened to release users' real names if the website didn't shut down – they followed through a month later, leaking 25 gigabytes of data.

13. Over four million users of adult content sites, such as Adult Friend Finder and Penthouse.com, had their account information stolen in 2016, including names, email addresses and passwords.

14. One of the US's largest credit bureaus, Equifax, experienced a data breach in 2017, in which over 200,000 customers' credit card data was vulnerable.

15. The 2013 data breach of Target Stores affected 110 million customers and caused the company's CIO and CEO to resign.

16. WellPoint, America's second-largest health insurer, had 78.8 million customers' personal information stolen in 2015. It was said to be the largest data breach in healthcare history.

17. In 2016, Uber paid a $100,000 bounty to hackers to get them to destroy the data they stole – 57 million Uber users and 600,000 drivers were affected.

18. The Democratic National Committee's email system was hacked in 2016. Nearly 20,000 emails were later published by WikiLeaks, having an impact on the presidential election campaign.

19. In May 2017, the WannaCry ransomware attack targeted computers running Microsoft Windows OS around the world. One of the largest agencies affected was the UK's National Health Service.

20. French presidential candidate Emmanuel Macron's campaign was threatened by the hack and leak of his emails two days before the election in 2017.

20 TRIALS THAT EVERYONE TALKED ABOUT

1. Martha Stewart's insider trading trial got wall-to-wall coverage in July 2004. The 'squeaky clean' businesswoman was sentenced to five months in prison.
2. The June 2005 trial of pop superstar Michael Jackson in Santa Barbara, California, USA, drew worldwide attention. Charged with molesting 13-year-old Gavin Arvizo, Jackson was acquitted on all charges. The 2019 documentary *Leaving Neverland* brought the issue of Jackson's behaviour into the public eye once again.
3. Five Iraqi judges tried the deposed president of Iraq, Saddam Hussein, for crimes against humanity. On 5 November 2006, he was sentenced to death by hanging.
4. Legendary music producer Phil Spector was prosecuted for the murder of actress Lana Clarkson and went on trial in 2007. A hung jury meant a 2009 retrial where he was found guilty.
5. Her crime might have just been violating her parole (following two drink-driving arrests in 2007), but 2.3 million people watched TMZ's live-stream of actress Lindsay Lohan's trial in 2010.
6. The trial of Casey Anthony, a Florida mother who was charged with murdering her two-year-old daughter, became an American national obsession in 2011. The jury took just 15 minutes to acquit her.
7. Michael Jackson's personal physician was the one on trial in 2011. Dr Conrad Murray was found guilty of involuntary manslaughter in the musician's death.
8. It was the white-collar crime that shocked the world – Kenneth Lay's and Jeffrey Skilling's massive securities, wire and accounting fraud brought down Enron. They were found guilty in 2006.
9. Former NFL star OJ Simpson's 1995 murder case was the 'trial of the century'. But despite being acquitted, he found himself back in the courtroom in 2007 after being charged with armed robbery and kidnapping. He was found guilty.

10. People tuned in from around the world in 2014 to watch celebrated South African sprinter Oscar Pistorius go on trial for the murder of his girlfriend, model Reeva Steenkamp.

11. The case of George Zimmerman for the shooting of Trayvon Martin in Florida, USA, culminated in the 2013 trial that saw Zimmerman claiming self-defence. After three weeks of testimony, the jury found Zimmerman innocent, leading to nationwide protests.

12. The American public were enthralled by the June 2004 to March 2005 trial of Scott Peterson. After 184 witnesses had testified in the murder of Peterson's pregnant wife Laci, he was found guilty.

13. In 2002, the former president of Yugoslavia, Slobodan Milošević, went on trial facing 66 counts of crimes against humanity, genocide and war crimes. The trial lasted until his death in 2006.

14. It was the same year that the Queen of England provided evidence in the theft trial of Princess Diana's former butler, Paul Burrell, leading to the case being dropped and the Royal family avoiding any further embarrassment.

15. In 2008, Steve Wright, a forklift truck driver, was found guilty on all charges for the murders of five women in Ipswich, England. He was jailed for life.

16. After the rape and murder of her friend Meredith Kercher in Italy, American student Amanda Knox became a media hate figure, branded Foxy Knoxy, and was wrongfully convicted twice for the crime.

17. In January 2018, Judge Rosemarie Aquilina allowed 156 women, who had accused former US Gymnastics team doctor Larry Nassar of sexually assaulting them, to provide victim impact statements in court. The powerful testimony was reported around the world.

18. The *News of the World* newspaper's Andy Coulson, Rebekah Brooks, Charlie Brooks and others went on trial in 2013 for charges relating to phone hacking.

19. In 2015, Netflix aired the hugely popular *Making a Murderer*, a documentary series charting the life of Steven Avery, including his 2007 conviction for the murder of Teresa Halbach.

20. There was international outrage in 2018 when Reuters journalists Wa Lone and Kyaw Soe were found guilty for breaching Myanmar's Official Secrets Acts for their reporting on a massacre of Rohingya Muslims.

20 EMBARRASSING BLUNDERS BY WORLD LEADERS

1. German Chancellor Gerhard Schröder made a faux pas of epic proportions in 2000 when he accidentally extinguished the eternal flame at Israel's Yad Vashem Holocaust Memorial.

2. In 2001, former American President Bill Clinton and his wife, Senator Hillary Diane Rodham Clinton, were criticised for taking $190,000 of furniture and furnishings when they left the White House.

3. Queen Elizabeth's husband Prince Philip was the subject of scrutiny in 2002 when, while on tour in Australia, he asked a successful Aboriginal businessman if the Aborigines still threw spears at each other.

4. In 2005, French President Jacques Chirac made a slight at the British when he told Russian President Vladimir Putin and Gerhard Schröder, 'You cannot trust people who have such bad cuisine.'

5. Following in his father's footsteps, Prince Charles was heard bad-mouthing the press during a 2005 photo call. He said: 'I hate doing this. And I hate these people.'

6. American President George W. Bush literally rubbed German Chancellor Angela Merkel up the wrong way when he tried to give her a shoulder massage during the 2006 G8 Summit.

7. At the same event, George W. Bush blundered again when he was caught on mic saying to Tony Blair, 'What they need to do is get Syria to get Hezbollah to stop doing this s—t.'

8. Gaff-prone former Italian Prime Minister Silvio Berlusconi drew criticism for his 2008 description of Barack Obama as 'young, handsome and also tanned.'

9. Journalist Katie Couric's 2008 interviews with American Vice Presidential candidate Sarah Palin were filled with damaging statements, particularly her failure to name a single newspaper or magazine she reads. She answered, instead: 'All of them, any of them that have been in front of me over all these years.'

10. In November the same year, shortly before the elections, Sarah Palin was the target of a prank call by the Masler Avengers, a Canadian comedy duo, pretending to be French President Nicolas Sarkozy.

11. In 2009, when the Obamas met with the British Royal Family, Michelle Obama broke protocol by throwing her arm around Queen Elizabeth II as they chatted, much to the shock of the media.

12. American Vice President Joe Biden put his foot in it in 2010 when he congratulated Obama on overhauling the healthcare system, saying, 'This is a big f—king deal.'

13. British Prime Minister Gordon Brown caused consternation when, whilst campaigning in the 2010 election, his microphone recorded him referring to a member of the public as a 'bigoted woman'.

14. When in China in 2010, British Prime Minister David Cameron annoyed the locals when he wore a Remembrance poppy – seen as a bitter reminder of the nineteenth-century Opium Wars the country lost to the British.

15. At the 2011 G20 summit, French President Nicolas Sarkozy and US President Barack Obama were overheard by the press criticising Israeli Prime Minister Benjamin Netanyahu.

16. In 2013, it emerged that there was video evidence of Toronto Mayor Rob Ford smoking crack cocaine – claims he would initially deny and then admit to.

17. At Nelson Mandela's memorial service, Barack Obama, David Cameron and Danish Prime Minister Helle Thorning-Schmidt were seen snapping a selfie.

18. In 2015, Australian Prime Minister Tony Abbott and his Immigration Minister Peter Dutton were caught on-mic making a joke about the rising sea levels in the South Pacific.

19. In 2015, on the American presidential campaign trail, Donald Trump mocked disabled *New York Times* reporter Serge Kovaleski, who suffers from a congenital condition.

20. Once he had been sworn in as president, Trump boasted about the size of his inauguration crowd, claiming it was the largest of its kind. It was a third of the size of President Obama's.

20 DEVASTATING TERRORIST ATTACKS

POLICE POLICE POLICE POLICE POLICE POLICE POLICE POLICE POLICE

1. On 11 September 2001, members of Islamic extremist group Al-Qaeda hijacked four passenger planes and carried out suicide attacks on the World Trade Center and the Pentagon in the United States.

2. A Moscow, Russia, theatre was the scene of a Chechen rebel siege in 2002, where 700 people were held hostage. When Russian forces stormed the building, 170 people lost their lives.

3. In 2002, two bombs exploded in a bar and a nightclub in the Kuta area of Bali, Indonesia: 202 people from 21 countries were killed.

4. In November 2003, four truck bomb attacks took place in Istanbul, Turkey, killing 57 people and injuring almost 700.

5. 2003 was also the year five bombs were targeted at Jewish people and westerners in Casablanca, Morocco. The 41 victims were mostly locals.

6. In 2004, 1,200 children and adults were held hostage at a school in Beslan, Russia, The Chechen rebels involved killed more than 330 people in the attack.

7. Three days before the Spanish general election of 2004, simultaneous bombings on the Madrid commuter train system killed 192 people.

8. Two days before Diwali in 2005, three blasts went off in Delhi, India, killing a total of 67 people.

9. On the morning of 7 July 2005, during rush hour, four bombs exploded across London on the transport network, killing 52 people.

POLICE POLICE POLICE POLICE POLICE

10. Mumbai, India, faced seven bomb blasts in just 11 minutes on its suburban railway on 11 July 2006. Over 200 people lost their lives.

11. Five synchronised bomb blasts across Delhi, India, killed over 20 people on 13 September 2008.

12. Mumbai, India, was the unfortunate target again in November 2008 when 10 Lashkar-e-Tayyiba terrorists killed 171 people in a coordinated attack on 12 locations.

13. In 2011, Anders Behring Breivik launched a deadly attack on Norway, including a bombing in Oslo with 8 fatally injured victims and a mass-shooting on Utoya Island where 69 young people died.

14. Taliban gunmen raided a military-run school in Pakistan in 2014, slaughtering 141 people, mostly students.

15. November 2015 saw a night of coordinated attacks in Paris, France, that included the Bataclan nightclub killing 130 people and injuring hundreds more.

16. Tunisia's tourist resort of Port El Kantaoui was the site of a mass shooting in June 2015, where 38 people, 30 of whom were British holidaymakers, were gunned down.

17. In July 2016, the Bastille Day celebrations in Nice, France, turned deadly when a terrorist drove a 19 tonne (18.7 ton) lorry into the crowd, killing more than 80 people.

18. Twenty-two people, many of whom were children, were killed and 116 injured in a bomb explosion at the Manchester Arena in England at the end of a 2017 Ariana Grande concert.

19. In 2017, 235 people were killed at a North Sinai mosque in Egypt when dozens of gunmen attacked the building with bombs and gunfire.

20. 2017 also saw three terrorists driving a van into pedestrians on London Bridge and launching knife attacks on people in cafes and shops around Borough Market in the UK capital. Eight people lost their lives.

POLICE POLICE POLICE POLICE POLIC

20 PLACES THAT CHANGED THEIR NAMES

1. In 2000, South Korea introduced the Revised Romanization of Korean, changing a number of place names' Romanised versions, including Inchŏn to Incheon, Kyŏngju to Gyeongju, and Pusan to Busan.

2. Since 1947, India has been renaming British imperial cities and states with localised ones. Calcutta was legally renamed Kolkata in 2001.

3. In 2001, an amendment was made to Canada's constitution to officially change the name of the province of Newfoundland to Newfoundland and Labrador.

4. East Timor, formerly Portuguese Timor, changed its name to Timor-Leste in 2002. 'Leste' is a Portuguese-derived term meaning 'east'.

5. South Africa's Northern Province changed its name to Limpopo in 2003 as well as the names of a number of its cities and towns...

6. ... One of these was the capital Pietersburg, which is now known as Polokwane. The new name means 'place of safety' in Northern Sotho.

~~Newfoundland~~
Newfoundland and Labrador

7. The New Jersey, USA, township of Buena Vista renamed its Richland township Mojito for two weeks in 2004, in honour of Bacardi rum – the area is a major East Coast supplier of mint.

8. In 2005, the hamlet of Santa, Idaho in the north-west United States changed its name to secretsanta.com for a year in a sponsorship deal.

9. Other Indian place names re-spelled in the twenty-first century include Pondicherry to Puducherry in 2006, Orissa to Odisha in 2011, and Bangalore to Bengaluru in 2007.

10. When NFL team the Pittsburgh Steelers made it to the Super Bowl in 2006, the Pennsylvania town of Washington voted to change its name to Steelers for a year.

~~Santa, Idaho~~ secretsanta.com

11 The break-up of Yugoslavia in the 1990s led to a number of new countries and name changes. In 2006 the State Union of Serbia and Montenegro became two separate countries.

12 In 2008, the Pakistani district of Nawabshah was renamed Shaheed Benazirabad in honour of assassinated former prime minister Benazir Bhutto.

13 In 2010, the capital city of Topeka, Kansas, USA, briefly changed its name to Google in order to be chosen as an experimental site for the company's ultra-fast broadband.

14 The Australian town of Speed changed its name to Speedkills in 2011 for one month as part of a road safety campaign.

15 The British town of Wootton Bassett became Royal Wootton Bassett in 2011, receiving a Royal Charter in recognition of its repatriation efforts for the UK's war dead.

16 Another British town name change came a year later when Staines changed its name to Staines-upon-Thames to promote its riverside location and improve its public image.

17 The island nation of Cape Verde changed its name to Cabo Verde in 2013. The name, meaning 'green cape', was given to it by Portuguese colonisers in 1444.

18 In 2016, it was decreed that the accepted short name for the Czech Republic would be Czechia, as opposed to the previously accepted Česká. In 2017, the Faculty of Sciences of Charles University in Prague set up a conference especially to assess the degree to which the new name had been adopted.

19 In 2018, King Mswati III changed his country's name of Swaziland to eSwatini, which essentially means 'land of the Swazis'.

20 Bangladesh decided to change the English spellings of five districts in 2018 to make them sound similar to the Bangla alphabet, including Barisal to Barishal and Chittagong to Chattogram.

20 OF THE MOST PIVOTAL MOVEMENTS, PROTESTS AND MARCHES

1. On 15 February 2003, one of the largest protests in human history took place when people in more than 600 cities opposed the imminent invasion of Iraq.
2. In 2004, the March for Women's Lives in Washington DC, USA, was one of the largest pro-choice protests in American history with an estimated 1.1 million attendees.
3. In 2004–2005, Ukrainians protested presidential election results on the grounds of corruption. Thousands demonstrated for three months in Kiev's Orange Revolution until a re-vote was ordered by the courts.
4. North India's Pink Sari movement started in 2007 protesting against violence aimed at women, oppression and child marriage. Led by the Gulabi Gang, an all-women vigilante group, they wear pink saris as a sign of strength.
5. Violent political protests gripped Thailand in 2010 when the 'Red Shirts' of the United Front for Democracy Against Dictatorship (UDD) called for the prime minister to dissolve parliament and hold new elections.
6. Around 200,000 people participated in Boobquake in 2010 at various locations around the US. The protest saw women wearing revealing clothing in response to comments by a leading Iranian Islamic authority who blamed immodestly dressed women for causing earthquakes.
7. Starting in Tunisia in 2010, the sometimes violent demonstrations of the Arab Spring saw leaders forced out of power as well as regime changes in Libya, Egypt, Syria and Bahrain.
8. Protests against global inequality and social injustice on Wall Street in 2011 led to the international Occupy movement, with occupation camps on every continent.
9. The same year saw European anti-austerity protests in Spain, Portugal and Ireland – the countries that were most heavily affected by the austerity measures introduced after the global financial crisis – in the light of growing national debts.

10. Students took to the streets of Chile between 2011 and 2013 demanding a new education framework and an end to private profiteering from higher education.

11. Changes to the election system introduced by the Chinese government saw crowds take to Hong Kong's streets in 2014. The umbrella became a solidarity symbol and an important defence mechanism against police pepper spray.

12. Mexico City's streets became a sea of black in 2014 after the government's response to the disappearance and probable massacre of 43 student teachers.

13. After President Vladimir Putin banned 'gay propaganda' in 2013, Russia's LGBTQ community organised and held mass protests ahead of the 2014 Winter Olympics in Sochi.

14. In 2013, 22 people lost their lives during a three-month series of protests in Istanbul, Turkey. Initially protesting against a shopping mall development, the people later called for press freedom and fair elections.

15. The Black Lives Matter street movement drew international recognition in 2014 after Michael Brown, an unarmed black teenager, was shot dead by a white policeman in the US town of Ferguson, Missouri.

16. In 2016, the Dakota Access Pipeline protests began, lasting almost a year, after construction was approved for a North American pipeline crossing the Standing Rock Indian Reservation.

17. After allegations of bribery, corruption and money laundering, 13 March 2016 saw nearly seven million Brazilians protest against Dilma Rousseff's government.

18. A day after President Donald Trump's inauguration, over 80 countries participated in the 2017 Women's March in support of human rights, immigration reform and environmental issues, among other things.

19. A global day of action was initiated by Rise for Climate on 8 September 2018. Events were held across 90 countries and seven continents – the largest single action on the issue of climate change.

20. In Britain an estimated 700,000 people took to the streets on 20 October 2018 to demand a People's Vote on the final terms of Britain's exit from the European Union. That makes it the second largest protest in the United Kingdom this century, coming behind the Stop the War demonstration in 2003.

People

20 Nobel Peace Prize Winners

1. The century's first Nobel Peace Prize winner was South Korean President Kim Dae-jung for his work on democracy and human rights both in his home country, particularly its relationship with North Korea, and in East Asia in general.

2. In 2001, the prize went to the United Nations and its Secretary-General Kofi Annan for their work towards a better organised and more peaceful world.

3. Former United States President Jimmy Carter was awarded the prize in 2002 in recognition of his 'untiring effort to find peaceful solutions to international conflicts, to advance democracy and human rights, and to promote economic and social development'.

4. In 2003, Iranian lawyer and former judge Shirin Ebadi was the recipient. As the founder of the Defenders of Human Rights Center in Iran she has focused especially on the struggle for the rights of women and children.

5. 2004's winner was Wangari Muta Maathai. The Kenyan environmental political activist was the first African woman to receive the prize. She died in 2011 from ovarian cancer.

6. The International Atomic Energy Agency of the United Nations won the award in 2005. The agency was set up in 1957 to promote the peaceful use of nuclear energy.

7. In 2006, Bangladeshi social entrepreneur Muhammad Yunus picked up the prize together with Grameen Bank for pioneering microcredit and microfinance to help advance economic and social opportunities for the world's poor.

8. Former American Vice President Al Gore was honoured in 2007 alongside the UN's Intergovernmental Panel on Climate Change. In 2006 Gore released *An Inconvenient Truth*, a book and Oscar-winning documentary about global warming.

9. Former President of Finland, Martti Ahtisaari, won the prize in 2008. He has twice worked to find a solution in Kosovo – 1999 and between 2005 and 2007 – and was involved in finding peaceful solutions for other conflicts such as those in Iraq, Northern Ireland and Central Asia.

10. When President Barack Obama won the award in 2009, there were mixed reactions from the international community, in large part because of the US's continuing military involvement in Iraq and Afghanistan.

11. Sometimes referred to as 'the Chinese Nelson Mandela', the 2010 prize went to writer and human rights activist Liu Xiaobo. He was a political prisoner at the time, making him the third incarcerated person to receive the award.

12. As the first elected female head of state in Africa, Liberian President Ellen Johnson Sirleaf, was a joint laureate winner in 2011.

13. She received the award alongside fellow female winners, Liberian peace activist Lemah Gbowee and Yemeni journalist Tawakkul Karman, the former was the first Arab woman to win the prize.

14. The European Union was recognised in 2012 for over 60 years of working towards 'the advancement of peace and reconciliation, democracy and human rights in Europe'.

15. Founded in 1997, the Organisation for the Prohibition of Chemical Weapons was the 2013 winner. The intergovernmental organisation has 193 member states and oversees the international effort to eliminate chemical weapons.

16. When Pakistani education activist Malala Yousafzai won the 2014 award together with Indian children's rights activist Kailash Satyarthi, she was 17 years old, making her the youngest ever recipient.

17. After the 2011 Tunisian Revolution, four organisations worked together to build a democracy in the country. The Tunisian National Dialogue Quartet was the 2015 laureate.

18. Juan Manuel Santos was President of Colombia in 2016 when he was the Prize's sole recipient. He was recognised for his efforts to bring the country's more than 50-year-long civil war to an end.

19. After the UN adopted the landmark Treaty on the Prohibition of Nuclear Weapons in 2017, the Nobel Peace Prize was awarded to the International Campaign to Abolish Nuclear Weapons which worked towards this goal.

20. In 2018, the award went to Congolese gynaecologist and pastor Denis Mukwege and Iraqi Yazidi human rights activist Nadia Murad for their work to end the use of sexual violence as a weapon of war.

20 ROYAL MARRIAGES AROUND THE WORLD

1. Monaco's 2011 shindig to celebrate the wedding of Prince Albert II and Olympic athlete Charlene Wittstock was compared to the 1956 wedding of his father Prince Rainier III and Hollywood actress Grace Kelly.

2. A 2005 civil ceremony at the Windsor Guildhall followed by a church service and prayer formalised the relationship between Britain's Prince Charles and Camilla Parker Bowles.

3. The year 2011 saw the much-anticipated wedding of Prince William and Catherine Middleton at Westminster Abbey in London. It was estimated that roughly half the British population watched at least parts of the televised broadcast.

4. Despite controversy over the familial relationship between the couple (they were double second cousins) an arranged marriage took place between Tongan Crown Prince Tupouto'a 'Ulukalala and Sinaitakala Fakafanua in 2012.

5. Copenhagen Cathedral was the setting for the 2004 wedding of Denmark's Crown Prince Frederik, to Australian former advertising executive Mary Donaldson. The couple met during the 2000 Sydney Olympic Games.

6. Prior to the 2012 wedding of Prince Guillaume of Luxembourg and Countess Stéphanie de Lannoy, the prince was the only unmarried heir apparent of a European monarchy.

7. Sweden has seen a succession of royal weddings, starting with Crown Princess Victoria of Sweden marrying her personal trainer Daniel Westling in 2010.

8. Then, in 2013, Princess Madeleine married American financier Christopher O'Neill. She had previously been planning a 2010 wedding to a Swedish lawyer, before the engagement was broken off.

9. As the last of the three children of the Swedish King Carl XVI Gustaf, Prince Carl Philip married former reality TV contestant and model, Sofia Hellqvist.

10. The live-streamed 2018 wedding of Britain's Prince Harry and American actress Meghan Markle sparked an international media frenzy, with a global viewing audience in the hundreds of millions.

11. Britain enjoyed its second royal wedding of 2018 when Princess Eugenie tied the knot with Jack Brooksbank, wine merchant and UK brand ambassador for George Clooney's Casamigos Tequila. Celebrity wedding guests included Naomi Campbell, Robbie Williams and Cara Delevinge.

12. In 2011, the 'Dragon King' of Bhutan married Jetsun Pema in the middle of a Punakha fortress. Bhutan held a three-day national holiday in the couple's honour.

13. Grace Kelly's grandson Prince Pierre tied the knot twice with Italian aristocrat Beatrice Borromeo in 2015. The bride wore five different dresses across the two celebrations.

14. The 27th Maharaja of the Kingdom of Mysore, Yaduveer Krishnadatta Chamaraja Wadiyar, wed his childhood friend and Dungapur royal, Trishika Kumari Singh, in 2016. There were 2,500 guests at the reception.

15. When Japanese Princess Sayako wed a commoner in 2005 – urban designer Yoshiki Kuroda – it marked the end of her royal status.

16. First in line to the Norwegian throne, Crown Prince Haakon, married a former waitress and single mother in 2001. For the occasion, the bride wore a veil that was 6.1 metres (20 feet) long.

17. The fairy-tale wedding of then Prince Willem-Alexander and Maxima Zorreguieta in 2002 featured a Valentino gown, a tiara and a horse-drawn carriage. They are now the King and Queen of the Netherlands.

18. One of the world's richest royals, the Sultan of Brunei, threw an extravagant week-long celebration for his daughter Princess Hajah and her husband-to-be, Pengiran Haji Muhammad Ruzaini, in 2012.

19. Queen Elizabeth II's granddaughter Zara Phillips married her rugby-star boyfriend Mike Tindall in 2011. They chose Edinburgh for the nuptials, making it the first royal wedding in Scotland for 20 years.

20. Islamic and Hindu traditions were combined for the 2013 wedding of Indonesia's HRH Princess Hayu and UN executive Kanjeng Pangeran Haryo Notonegoro.

20 NOTABLE CELEBRITY BREAK-UPS

1. Meg Ryan and Dennis Quaid were married in 1991. After she had an affair with *Proof of Life* co-star Russell Crowe, the couple announced their separation in 2000.

2. Actors Tom Cruise and Nicole Kidman co-starred in three films and were married in 1990. After adopting two children together, they ended their relationship in 2001.

3. Chris Martin and Gwyneth Paltrow announced their separation after more than a decade of marriage in 2014. They made headlines for saying they were 'consciously uncoupling'.

4. 2004 was the year singer and actress Jennifer Lopez ended a relationship with Ben Affleck and married long-time friend and singer Marc Anthony. However, the two divorced ten years later.

5. Ten years of marriage and three children couldn't hold Hollywood sweethearts Jennifer Garner and Ben Affleck together. They announced their separation in 2015 before rumours of Affleck's affair with the nanny surfaced.

6. No Doubt front-woman Gwen Stefani and Bush lead singer and guitarist Gavin Rossdale met in 1995. Twenty years later Stefani filed for divorce citing 'irreconcilable differences'.

7. *Keeping Up With The Kardashians* mastermind and mom-boss Kris Jenner and Caitlyn Jenner, then Bruce, announced their separation in 2013. In 2015, Caitlyn Jenner came out as transgender.

8. Model and TV presenter Heidi Klum got engaged to musician Seal in 2004 – on a glacier in British Columbia, Canada. They renewed their vows every year until 2012 when they announced their divorce.

9. Mariah Carey and Nick Cannon married in 2008. They announced their separation in 2014, just three years after the birth of their twins.

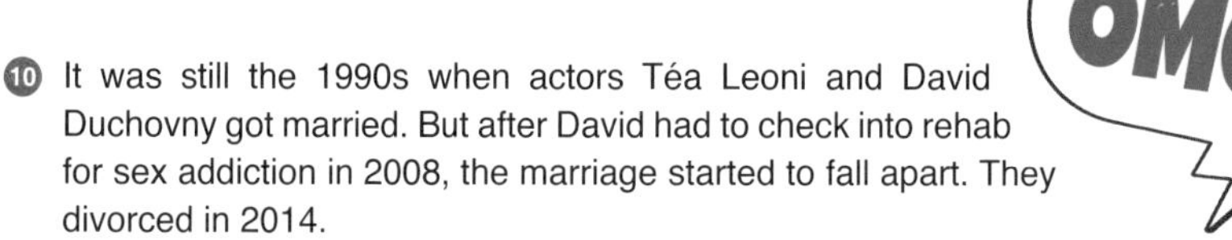

10. It was still the 1990s when actors Téa Leoni and David Duchovny got married. But after David had to check into rehab for sex addiction in 2008, the marriage started to fall apart. They divorced in 2014.

11. After just 72 days of marriage, reality TV star Kim Kardashian filed for divorce from NBA player Kris Humphries in 2011. Their wedding was shown in a TV special on the American pay television channel *E!*

12. British actor Orlando Bloom and Australian supermodel Miranda Kerr got married in 2010, had a baby in 2011, and announced their separation in 2013.

13. Katie Holmes got engaged to Tom Cruise after seven weeks of dating. In 2006, she became his third wife, but filed for divorce after five-and-a-half years of marriage.

14. Comedian Russell Brand and singer Katy Perry's extravagant 2010 wedding took place in Rajasthan, India. After just over a year of marriage, Brand filed for divorce.

15. Hollywood A-listers Robin Wright and Sean Penn's on-again, off-again relationship spanned nearly 20 years. It finally came to an end in 2010 when their divorce was finalised.

16. In 2008, Heather Mills asked for a £125 million divorce pay-out from husband Paul McCartney, who she had married in 2002 and has a daughter with. After a very public hearing, she received money and assets worth £23.4 million.

17. When film director Guy Ritchie and Madonna divorced in 2008, the terms granted Ritchie over £50 million, making it one of the largest divorce settlements in British history.

18. Brad Pitt and Jennifer Aniston were Hollywood's golden couple. After a top-secret wedding ceremony in Malibu, California, in 2000, they divorced just five years later.

19. Pitt was at the centre of another marital break-up in 2016, when his divorce from Angelina Jolie was finalised. The couple had been together since 2005.

20. Reese Witherspoon met Ryan Phillippe at her 21st birthday party, and they married in 1999. The couple, who starred in *Cruel Intentions* together, separated in 2006.

20 Music Legends Who Died

1. Whitney Houston was found face down in a water-filled bathtub in her Beverly Hilton hotel room in 2012. Her death was deemed an 'accident'.

2. Michael Jackson's death was ruled a homicide by the Los Angeles County Coroner in 2009. His personal physician Conrad Murray was convicted for involuntary manslaughter in 2011.

3. After a long and public battle with alcohol and drug abuse, Amy Winehouse was found dead by accidental alcohol poisoning in her home in 2011.

4. American singer Etta James died in 2012, just before her 74th birthday. She had suffered from Alzheimer's disease and terminal leukaemia.

5. David Bowie battled liver cancer for 18 months before he died in 2016. His death came two days after the release of *Blackstar,* his 25th studio album.

6. Prince also died in 2016. He was found unresponsive in an elevator at his home after taking an accidental overdose of the opioid painkiller fentanyl. He was 57 years old.

7. On Christmas morning that same year, George Michael was found dead in his bed by his Australian partner Fadi Fawaz. He had died of natural causes.

8. Grammy-award-winning artist Aaliyah died in 2001. She was on board a twin-engine aircraft that crashed shortly after take-off from the Bahamas and exploded with her on board. She was 22 years old.

9. In 2002, Lisa 'Left Eye' Lopes, a member of the American girl group TLC, died at the age of 30 after suffering a severe head trauma and neck injuries in a car accident.

10. Aretha Franklin was 76 when she died in 2018. A Homegoing Service was held in Detroit and streamed live by news agencies. Performances were given by Ariana Grande, Jennifer Hudson and Stevie Wonder.

11. Four months after his wife's death, Johnny Cash passed away from diabetes complications in 2003. The couple had been married for 35 years.

12. Ray Charles was 73 and had acute liver disease when he died in 2004. His final album was released posthumously and received eight Grammy Awards.

13. Bee Gees band member Maurice Gibb died unexpectedly in 2003 because his bowel and small intestine had become so twisted they restricted his blood flow. He was only 53 years old.

14. When Beatle George Harrison died in 2001, he was 58 and had battled lung and brain cancer. He spent time with bandmates Ringo Starr and Paul McCartney a few weeks before his death.

15. Peggy Lee's career spanned six decades – she even performed from a wheelchair in the 1990s. She passed away in 2002, at the age of 81.

16. In 2005, Luther Vandross died of a heart attack when he was 54 years old. The year before he had been awarded a Grammy for Song of the Year for 'Dance with My Father'.

17. Five-time-Grammy-winner Donna Summer died aged 63 in 2012. She suffered from lung cancer.

18. As one of the most influential blues musicians of all time, B. B. King's death in 2015 brought thousands of people to the streets of Memphis, Tennessee, USA, to pay their respects.

19. After falling and suffering a stroke while holidaying at her Spanish villa, Cilla Black died in 2015. The day after her funeral a compilation of her hits became her first UK number one album.

20. 1970s heartthrob David Cassidy was hospitalised in 2017 with liver and kidney failure. He died before doctors were able to perform a liver transplant operation.

20 Children Who Made a Difference

1. In 2012, 15-year-old Malala Yousafzai was riding the bus home from school in Swat District, north-west Pakistan, when she was shot in the head by a Taliban gunman. She survived and went on to become an international activist for female education and a Nobel peace prize winner.
2. Photos of three-year-old Alan Kurdi's dead body, washed up on a Turkish beach in 2015, sparked an international outcry about the Syrian refugee crisis.
3. When Alexandra Scott died from cancer in 2004, aged just eight years old, she had already raised $1 million for cancer research. Her work lives on through the Alex's Lemonade Stand Foundation.
4. Called a modern Anne Frank, the seven-year-old Syrian refugee, Bana al-Abed, started tweeting about her life in war-torn Aleppo in 2016. Her English-speaking mother helped her document her life on Twitter and in a book called *'Dear World'*, the phrase she starts her tweets with.
5. In 2007, a six-year-old Jazz Jennings was interviewed by Barbara Walters about being a transgender child. She has become a prominent LGBTQ activist.
6. The 11-year-old Canadian singer and children's activist Capri Everitt received a Guinness World Record in 2016 for 'most national anthems sung in their host countries in one year'. She travelled to 80 countries (76 counted for the record), sang each anthem in its own language and raised awareness for orphaned children.
7. At the 2016 Rio de Janeiro Olympic Games, 18-year-old Yusra Mardini, who had helped push a boat across the Aegean Sea for hours when she fled Syria with her family, was part of the first refugee team. The swimmer competed in the 100-metres freestyle and butterfly events.
8. After her father, conservationist Steve Irwin, died tragically in 2006, when she was just eight years old, Australian Bindi Irwin continued his legacy, encouraging young people to take an interest in wildlife.
9. Canadian Ryan Hreljac was just ten years old when he founded Ryan's Well Foundation in 2001 to build wells in Africa. In 2015, the Foundation's 1,000th well was built.
10. Ann Makosinski's body-heat-powered flashlight was her entry to the Google Science Fair in 2013. The 15-year-old wanted to find a way to provide light to those who cannot afford electricity in their homes. Her invention won her a $25,000 scholarship for the 15–16 age category and a 'once-in-a-lifetime experience' from CERN (the European Organization for Nuclear Research), LEGO or Google.

11. At just 16 years of age, Dutch teenager Boyan Slat came up with a system that makes plastic concentrate itself in water, helping with ocean clean-up. In November 2014, at the age of 20, he became the youngest recipient of the UN's Champions of the Earth Award.

12. Colorado-born Easton LaChapelle was just 14 years old when, in 2013, he entered a school science fair with a robotic hand made from LEGO, fishing wire and electrical tubing. The self-taught young inventor went on to create 3D printed, mind-controlled RoboArm prosthetics for a fraction of conventional costs and his company Unlimited Tomorrow now works together with tech giants like Microsoft and NASA.

13. In 2009, Anoyara Khatun was a victim of child trafficking in India. She was rescued by Save the Children and later returned to West Bengal to help put a stop to the practice. At 21 years old she became one of the youngest women to win the Indian 'Women Power Award', supporting her aim to stop children from being exploited.

14. Nkosi Johnson was born HIV-positive and helped to change the public's perception of HIV/AIDS in the 1990s. In 2000, aged 11, he gave the keynote speech at the 13th International AIDS Conference. He died the following year.

15. Sixteen-year-old Zambian Thandiwe Chama won the International Children's Peace Prize in 2007 for her work as an educational rights activist.

16. In 2015, indigenous environmental activist Xiuhtezcatl Martinez was one of 22 young people who filed a lawsuit against the US federal government arguing that, by ignoring climate change, the government is denying them their constitutional rights.

17. By 2018, 13-year-old Mikaila Ulmer's Me & The Bees Lemonade was selling 360,000 bottles per year. She started the business to help save the bees at the age of four.

18. Yash Gupta was 2013 CNN Young Wonder Hero In 2010, when he was just 14 years old, Gupta founded Sight Learning. By 2019, this non-profit organisation had collected over 60,000 pairs of glasses and raised $1.8 million to give glasses to children who otherwise couldn't afford them.

19. Swedish climate activist Greta Thunberg went on strike from school to raise awareness of global warming. The 15-year-old also addressed leaders at the 2018 UN climate conference in Katowice, Poland.

20. Eighteen-year-old American student Emma González was one of a number of teenagers who called for stricter gun control laws after they survived a high-school shooting in Florida, USA, in 2018.

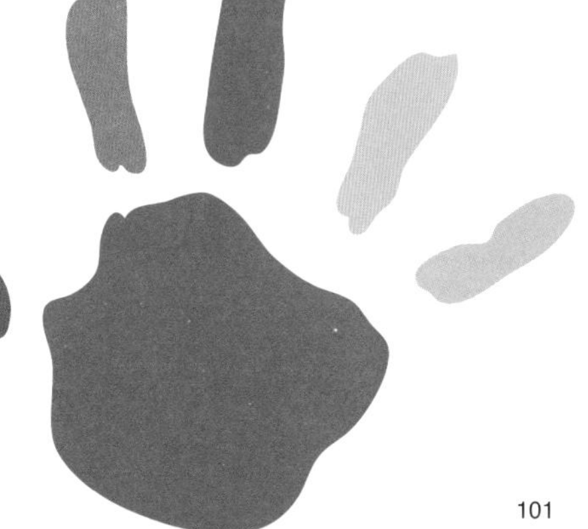

20 FEMALE BILLIONAIRES

1. Dutch billionaire Charlene de Carvalho-Heineken inherited 23 per cent of the Heineken business in 2002 from her father. In 2018 she was worth $15.8 billion.

2. In 2004, Rahel Blocher's father sold his shares in Swiss polymer and chemical company EMS-Chemie to his children. She has since become Switzerland's richest woman.

3. In 2017, Francoise Bettencourt Meyers' mother died. As her sole heiress, the 68-year-old inherited the L'Oréal family fortune of $39.5 billion. In 2018 she was named the world's second wealthiest women by *Forbes*.

4. The wealthiest woman of 2018 was named as Alice Walton, heiress to the Walmart fortune. In 2016, she owned $11 billion in Walmart shares. She had joined *Forbes*' top ten World's Billionaires list in 2001.

5. Alice's mother, Helen, was also on the list until her death in 2007. At that time, she had an estimated net worth of $16.4 billion.

6. Beloved author of the Harry Potter series, among other works, J. K. Rowling has conjured a fortune of around $1 billion, as of 2019.

7. In 2012, businesswoman Wu Yajun was the richest woman in China. She made her fortune in Longfor Properties. In 2018, her fortune was estimated at $2.9 billion.

8. In 2007, when she was just 26, Yang Huiyan's father transferred a large part of her 57 per cent stake in real estate developer Country Garden Holdings to her. In 2018 she was worth $21.9 billion.

9. In 2018, the world's youngest billionaire was Alexandra Andresen, aged 22. In 2007, both she and her sister Katharina, inherited 42.2 per cent of Norwegian investment company, Ferd. In 2018, despite her $1.4 billion fortune, she only ranked 1,650th in the world.

10. In 2011, on the death of her husband, Steve Jobs, Laurene Powell Jobs inherited his Trust, which included a stake in the Walt Disney Company and 38.5 million Apple Inc. shares.

11. Australia's wealthiest person, and the world's seventh richest woman, is mining billionaire Gina Rhinehart. Her fortune jumped from $2 billion to $9 billion in 2011.

12. In 2013, Spanish billionaire Sandra Ortega Mera inherited her $6.9 billion fortune from her mother Rosalia Mera, who cofounded Inditex, the company behind Zara clothes stores.

13. Pollyanna Chu saw her Hong Kong-based Kingston Financial Group wealth grow from $1 billion in 2013 to $7 billion in 2018.

14. Fidelity Investments made American Abigail Johnson CEO in 2014. The privately held mutual fund was founded by her grandfather, and she owns 24.5 per cent of it.

15. Susanne Klatten is the richest woman in Germany – she inherited her wealth from her father in the 1980s and from her mother in 2015. She owns chemical company Altana and 19.2 per cent of BMW – and in 2018 she was worth $25 billion.

16. In 2015, Maria Franco Fissolo, aged 81, was the world's 32nd richest person with a fortune of $23.4 billion. She is the widow of Michele Ferroro, who built the business behind Nutella, Kinder and Tic Tac.

17. In 2016, Jacqueline Mars, granddaughter of Mars founder Franklin Clarence Mars, was worth $27 billion, owning a third of the confectionery business. She has worked for the family business for 20 years.

18. The richest Indian woman, as of 2018, was Savitri Jindal, with a net worth of $8.8 billion. Her husband, O. P. Jindal, who was the founder of multi-faceted Jindal Group, died in a helicopter crash in 2005.

19. In 2017, co-CEO of online gambling company Bet365, Denise Coates, paid herself $279 million, making her the highest-paid British CEO that year, and the world's best-paid female CEO.

20. Hong Kong's Zhou Qunfei is one of the world's richest self-made women, with $7.8 billion in 2018. She started out as a teenage migrant factory worker – and now chairs smartphone screen supplier Lens Technology.

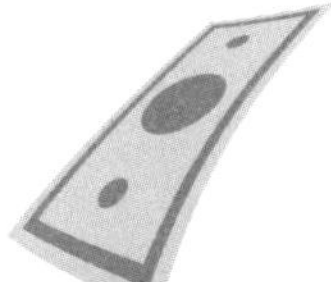

20 PEOPLE WHOSE CONVICTIONS WERE OVERTURNED

1. The 2000 Good Friday Agreement saw the release of Provisional IRA member and explosives specialist Bernard McGinn, who was sentenced to 490 years in prison in 1999 for 34 offences, including the murder of British soldiers.
2. Sally Clark, a solicitor who was jailed in 1999 for the murder of her two sons, spent three years in prison before her conviction was overturned on appeal in the UK in 2003.
3. Discredited evidence given by the same paediatrician as in Clark's case also helped to overturn Angela Cannings' conviction, among others, in 2003. A year before, she'd also been sentenced to life imprisonment for the murder of her two sons.
4. Royal Navy sailor Michael Shirley was convicted of the murder of Linda Cook in Portsmouth, UK, in 1988. He was in prison until 2003 when his conviction was quashed because DNA extracted from semen samples recovered at the crime scene proved not to be his.
5. Canadian Steven Truscott was just 14 in 1959 when he was sentenced to death for the rape and murder of his 12-year-old classmate Lynne Harper, before the judge changed the sentence to life imprisonment. He served 10 years, but had to wait another 38 before, in 2007, the Ontario Court of Appeal overturned his conviction after re-examining forensic evidence.
6. Hamed Zinati spent four years in prison in Israel after being convicted of murder in 2007. The Israeli Supreme Court overturned his conviction on appeal and awarded him $100,000 in compensation.
7. In 2001, Barry George was convicted of the murder of British TV presenter Jill Dando. It was a high-profile case, but the Court of Appeal found the conviction unsafe and it was quashed in 2007. A retrial led to his acquittal in 2008.
8. The longest miscarriage of justice case in British history involved the murder of Teresa Elena De Simons in 1979 and the conviction of the 34-year-old Sean Hodgson in 1982. He served 27 years in prison before DNA analysis led to his exoneration and release in March 2009. Hodgson died 3 years later.
9. Paediatric nurse Lucia de Berk was sentenced to life imprisonment in the Netherlands in 2003 for the murder of four patients in her care and three attempted murders. She was exonerated in 2010.
10. In 2009, Italian Raffaele Sollecito and American Amanda Knox were both sentenced to 26 years for the murder of UK student Meredith Kercher. They appealed successfully and were released in 2011. In 2014 the initial guilty verdict was reinstated and it took another year before the Italian Supreme court exonerated them. Rudy Guede is serving a 16-year sentence for the murder.

11. Juan Rivera Jr. was awarded $20 million in a wrongful conviction lawsuit – the largest settlement of this kind in US history after his initial conviction for the rape and murder of 11-year-old Holly Staker in 1992 was overturned in 2011.

12. Brian Banks spent more than five years in prison for the rape of a fellow high-school student, Wanetta Gibson. She later admitted to fabricating the story, and in 2012 his conviction was overturned. He went on to sign as line-backer for the Atlanta Falcons NFL team.

13. The 2001 murder of *Columbia Daily Tribune* sports editor Kent Heitholt resulted in the wrongful conviction of 27-year-old Ryan Ferguson in 2005. He spent almost ten years in prison, before the two key witnesses recanted their testimony and he was finally released in 2013.

14. English footballer Ched Evans was convicted of rape in 2012. The professional footballer spent two-and-a-half years in prison before his conviction was quashed by the Court of Appeal in 2016. A second trial found him not guilty.

15. Indiana State Policeman David Camm spent 2000 to 2013 in prison after being twice wrongfully convicted for murdering his wife and two children. His third trial resulted in acquittal, by which time the state had spent $4.5 million prosecuting him.

16. American Adrian Thomas's coerced confession was used to convict him of the second-degree murder of his four-month-old son in 2009. It was thrown out on appeal in 2014, and a second trial found Thomas not guilty. He was subsequently released.

17. Australian Henry Keogh served 21 years of a 26-year sentence for the 1994 murder of his fiancée. The conviction was overturned in 2014.

18. Former Irish rugby player David Tweed was convicted in 2012 for gross indecency, indecent assault of two young girls and inciting gross indecency. His conviction was quashed in 2016.

19. In 2017, Isaac Wright Jr became the first person to be condemned to life imprisonment, secure his own release and exoneration, and then be granted a law license by the same court that sentenced him.

20. In 2000, Tomasz Komenda plead guilty to the rape and murder of a teenage girl that happened on New Year's Eve 1996/1997. In 2018 new evidence emerged and Komenda's conviction was overturned. He had spent 6,540 days in prison

20 Famous Births

1. Madonna and director husband Guy Ritchie welcomed Rocco into the world in 2000 a month early. The musician had caused controversy for saying that British hospitals were unfit for her to give birth in.

2. Celebrity baby names became the thing of tabloid delight and derision in 2004 when actress Gwyneth Paltrow and Coldplay frontman Chris Martin named their daughter Apple.

3. Jon and Kate Gosselin's sextuplets (plus their older twin sisters) became an American sensation in 2005, shortly after their birth. The family's daily life was broadcast on TLC.

4. Angelina Jolie and Brad Pitt's first biological child, Shiloh Nouvel, came into the world in 2006. The couple donated $4.1 million, paid to them by *People* magazine for photos of the baby, to help African children.

5. When *Vanity Fair* came out in October 2006 there was a 60 per cent sales spike – everyone wanted to catch a glimpse of Tom Cruise and Katie Holmes' six-month-old daughter Suri.

6. Singer and actress Jennifer Lopez and Marc Anthony welcomed twins in February 2008: Maximilian and Emme. The babies appeared in the March issue of *People,* costing the magazine $6 million.

7. In August 2008, Angelina Jolie gave birth to her and Brad Pitt's twins Knox and Vivienne. *People* and *Hello!* magazines paid $14 million to secure the first photos of the babies. The money went to a foundation created by the couple that largely focuses on helping children around the world.

8. After she was chosen as the Republican vice-presidential candidate in 2008, Sarah Palin revealed her teenage daughter was five months pregnant with her first grandchild. Baby Tripp was born a month after the election in December.

9. *Sex and the City* star Sarah Jessica Parker and actor husband Matthew Broderick became the parents of twin girls, Marion and Tabitha, using a surrogate mother in 2009.

10. 2011 was the year the Beckham clan grew once again when former Spice Girl and fashion designer Victoria and footballer David added daughter Harper to their brood of three boys.

11. Mariah Carey and husband Nick Cannon became parents to twins, Moroccan and Monroe, in 2011. According to reports, Cannon was so nervous he went to the wrong department at the hospital.

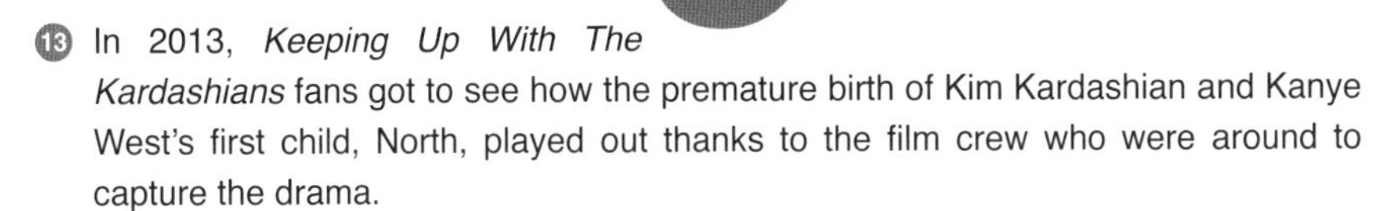

12. Fans waited excitedly to hear about the birth of Beyoncé and Jay-Z's daughter Blue Ivy, who arrived into the world in January 2012.

13. In 2013, *Keeping Up With The Kardashians* fans got to see how the premature birth of Kim Kardashian and Kanye West's first child, North, played out thanks to the film crew who were around to capture the drama.

14. It was the same year the world's media awaited the birth of Prince William and Catherine Middleton's first baby, Prince George, who was welcomed by 21-gun salutes in Bermuda, New Zealand, Canada and the UK.

15. The birth of his sister, Charlotte, who was born two years later, generated similar public interest. Tower Bridge and the London Eye were illuminated pink in her honour.

16. December 2015 was the month Facebook billionaire Mark Zuckerberg and his wife paediatrician Priscilla Chan, announced to the world that their first child, Max, had been born. Chan had previously experienced three miscarriages.

17. 2017 was the year of twins: Beyoncé and Jay-Z had a pair (Sir and Rumi), Madonna adopted a couple (Esther and Stella), and Amal and George Clooney became parents for the first time when Ella and Alexander were born.

18. *Keeping Up With The Kardashians* star Kylie Jenner managed to keep her pregnancy a secret from the press, announcing she had given birth to a baby girl, Stormi, in February 2018.

19. She wasn't the only Kardashian to have a baby that year, either. Khloé welcomed her first child, True, in April, and a surrogate delivered Kim's third baby Chicago a month earlier.

20. Another royal birth almost stole the limelight from Prince Harry and Meghan Markle's wedding, when Prince Louis was born to the Duke and Duchess of Cambridge in April 2018, a few weeks before his uncle tied the knot.

20 SPORTS SCANDALS

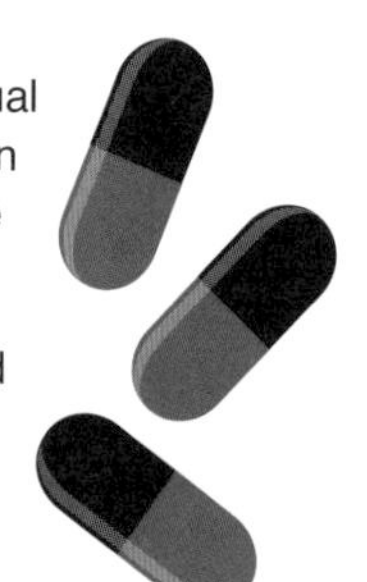

1. After the 2000 Summer Paralympics in Sydney, Spain's ID (intellectual disabilities) basketball team were stripped of their gold medals when it came to light that most of the players had not undergone the medical tests to ensure they had an intellectual disability.

2. Little League pitcher Danny Almonte could throw a ball at a speed of 76 mph (122 kph), but in 2001 after leading his team to a third-place finish in the Little League World Series, it was revealed he was two years too old to compete as a junior baseballer.

3. Before the 2002 Salt Lake City Winter Olympics started, it was already mired in scandal after it emerged that members of the International Olympic Committee took bribes from the city's organising officials during the bidding process.

4. And then during the competition, it came to light that the pairs' figure skating competition had been fixed by the judges. The end result was that two pairs, from Russia and Canada, received gold medals.

5. Kobe Bryant was arrested in 2003 for sexually assaulting a woman. The married NBA star admitted to a consensual sexual encounter with the woman, damaging his public image, but the case was later dropped.

6. American cyclist Floyd Landis's miraculous turnaround in Stage 17 of the 2006 Tour de France invited suspicion. Immediately after he tested positive for banned synthetic testosterone.

7. In 2006, it emerged that NFL draft second pick, Reggie Bush, had received gifts and money from sports agents, in violation of National Collegiate Athletic Association policies. He eventually was stripped of his prestigious Heisman Trophy title.

8. New England Patriots' head coach, Bill Belichick, was fined $500,000 in 2007 for videotaping another team's defensive coaches during an NFL game, in violation of league rules, in an incident known as 'Spygate'.

9. Rugby Union fans were shocked to learn that during the quarter final of the 2009 Heineken Cup (and on four previous occasions), Harlequins' Tom Williams had faked a blood injury to facilitate tactical substitutions.

10. After winning the Tour de France seven times, Lance Armstrong was named by the United States Anti-Doping Agency as the ringleader of a sophisticated doping programme in 2012. He was stripped of all his medals from 1998 onward.

11. More scandal sullied the NBA in 2007 when referee Tim Donaghy resigned. He then pleaded guilty to two federal charges related to an FBI investigation that found he had bet on games in which he had officiated.

12. Michael Vick's NFL career was put on hold in 2007 when the Atlanta Falcons quarterback pleaded guilty to being involved in a dog fighting ring. He spent 21 months in a federal prison.

13. In December 2009, more than a dozen women came forward claiming they had had affairs with married pro golfer Tiger Woods. He later admitted to a number of infidelities in a televised statement and lost several lucrative sponsorship deals as a result.

14. A number of officials at football's governing body, FIFA, faced charges after an FBI investigation into wire fraud, money laundering and racketeering resulted in multiple arrests in 2015.

15. Professional baseballer Barry Bonds was indicted on four counts of perjury in 2007 in relation to evidence he gave under oath to a Grand Jury investigating steroid use in 2003.

16. In 2013, during the off-season, New England Patriots tight end Aaron Hernandez was arrested and charged for the murder of Odin Lloyd. He was found guilty two years later and sentenced to life imprisonment.

17. A two-year grand jury investigation led to the 2011 arrest and charge of long-time Penn State football coach Jerry Sandusky for 52 counts of sexual abuse of young boys.

18. In 2016, the International Association of Athletics Federations gave lifetime bans to the former head of Russian athletics. A number of athletes were banned from competing in the Rio de Janeiro Summer Olympics after accusations of a state-sanctioned doping programme.

19. British football was rocked by the sexual abuse allegations that started to emerge in 2016. In the years that followed a number of former youth coaches and football staff faced criminal prosecutions.

20. Operation Slapshot was the name given to a New Jersey, USA, police operation that brought down an illegal gambling ring in 2006. It involved Phoenix Coyotes coach Rick Tocchet and a number of NHL players.

20 WORLD RECORDS IN ATHLETICS

1. 2005 was the year the Memorial Van Damme event in Brussels saw Ethiopian long-distance runner Kenenisa Bekele smash nearly three seconds off the men's 10,000-metre world record, which now stands at 26 minutes, 17.53 seconds.

2. The women's javelin throw world record was broken in 2000, 2005 and again in 2008 when Czech athlete Barbora Špotáková threw a distance of 72.28 metres.

3. The current women's 5,000-metre record of 14:11.15 was set at the Bislett Games in Oslo in 2008 by double Olympic gold medallist Tirunesh Dibaba.

4. In the final of the World Athletics Championship in 2009, in front of a Berlin crowd, Usain Bolt underpinned his status as fastest man on Earth, when he broke his own record to run the 100 metres in 9.58 seconds.

5. Four days later he ran in the final of the 200-metres event, in which he bettered his own 2008 record by 0.11 seconds.

6. Kenya's David Rudisha broke his own men's 800-metres world record for the third time in a row at the 2012 London Olympic Games, when he finished in 1:40.91.

7. The London Olympics were also the stage for the record-breaking men's 4 x 100 metres relay team from Jamaica. Nesta Carter, Michael Frater, Yohan Blake and Usain Bolt finished in 36.84 seconds.

8. Men's 20,000-metre records were recorded on the track by Haile Gebrselassie in 2007 (56:26.0) and by Zersenay Tadese on the road in 2010 at the Lisbon Half Marathon (55:21).

9. The men's 400-metres world record had been held by Michael Johnson for 17 years before South Africa's Wayde van Niekerk broke it with 43.03 at the 2016 Rio de Janeiro Olympics.

10. The fastest marathon on record at the time of writing was completed in 2018 by Kenyan Olympic champion Eliud Kipchoge in 2:01.39 in Berlin.

11. The women's record is still held by British runner Paula Radcliffe, who won the London Marathon in 2003 in a time of 2:15.25.

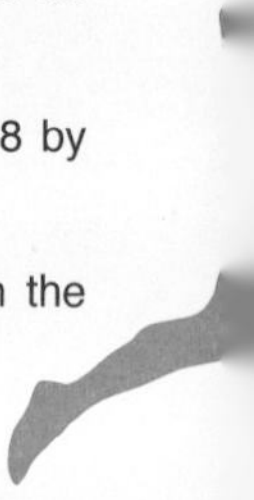

12. In 2014, the French gold medallist of the London Olympic Games, Renaud Lavillenie, broke the pole vault record of 21 years (set by Sergey Bubka in 1993 at 6.15 metres). Lavillenie cleared a height of 6.16 metres in Bubka's home town Donetsk, Ukraine.

13. The women's world record had been set a few years before by Russia's Yelena Isinbayeva, the first woman to break the 5-metre barrier. Her record-breaking 2009 vault was 5.06 metres.

14. When Ethiopia's Genzebe Dibaba broke the women's 1,500-metre record in 2015 in Monaco, it ended an over two-decade reign for Chinese runner Yunxia Qu.

15. In 2017, Dibaba also shaved 2 seconds off the 24-year-old 2,000-metres record of 5:25.36, run in 1993 by Ireland's Sonia O'Sullivan. The new best time is 5:23.75.

16. Women's long-distance saw another 1993 record broken, this time at the Rio de Janeiro Olympics in 2016, when Almaz Ayana ran the 10,000 metres in 29:17.45.

17. The long-running 100-metres hurdles record of 12.21, set by Yordanka Donkova in 1988, was finally broken by the USA's Kendra Harrison when she hurdled in 12.20 at the London Müller Anniversary Games in 2016.

18. And the women's half-marathon record was broken twice in 2017, first by Peres Jepchirchir in February in Ras al-Khaimah, UAE, and then in October by fellow Kenyan Joyciline Jepkosgei, when she ran a time of 1:04.51 at the World Half Marathon Championships in Valencia, Spain.

19. In Columbia, Missouri in 2005, Lithuania's Austra Skujytė, who also competes in heptathlon, broke the women's decathlon world record with a score of 8,358.

20. Poland's Anita Włodarczyk became the first woman to throw the hammer over 80 metres when she achieved an 82.98-metre throw in 2016. She was the Olympic gold medallist in London, 2012, and Rio de Janeiro, Brazil, 2016.

20 MOST EXPENSIVE FOOTBALL TRANSFERS

1. When Brazilian footballer Neymar moved from Barcelona to Paris Saint-Germain in 2017 he more than doubled the existing world record for the biggest transfer fee ever. The Paris club paid £198 million (€222 million).

2. Meanwhile Ousmane Dembélé had arrived in the Spanish city of Barcelona from Dortmund for £97 million (€105 million), making the forward the joint second most expensive footballer at the time.

3. That title was held with 2016 transfer Paul Pogba who returned to Manchester United after four years at Juventus in 2016 for a record £89 million (€105 million). Juventus only paid £500,000 for him in 2012.

4. Paris Saint-Germain flashed the cash again in 2018 when they paid Monaco £158 million (€180 million) for the then 18-year-old Kylian Mbappé, making him the most expensive teenage player so far. Mbappé was only the second teenager after Pele to score in a World Cup final, winning the 2018 tournament with France.

5. Philippe Coutinho made the move from Liverpool for £106 million (€120 million), signing a five-and-a-half-year contract with a hefty buy-out clause in 2018.

6. In 2018, Portuguese superstar Cristiano Ronaldo said farewell to Real Madrid and joined Italy's Juventus in the biggest transfer paid by an Italian club and the most paid for a player over 30: £88.5 million (€100 million).

7. Ronaldo had previously held the record in 2009 when he was sold by Manchester United to the Spanish team for £80 million (€94 million).

8. Welsh player Gareth Bale broke the world transfer record at the time when he moved to Real Madrid for £86 million (€100 million) in 2013. He still holds the record for the most expensive British player.

9. The 2016 move of the Argentine's striker Gonzalo Higuaín from Napoli to Juventus for £75.3 million (€90 million) was the highest domestic transfer in Italy.

10. When Romelu Lukaku moved from Everton to Manchester United in 2017, the £75 million (€85 million) paid made him the club's second most expensive signing after Paul Pogba.

11 This was the same amount Barcelona had paid for Luis Suárez in 2014 after his nine-match ban for biting in the World Cup. It was the most ever paid for a South American player at the time and still the fourth highest at the time of writing.

12 And the cheque also matched this when Virgil van Dijk headed north from Southampton to Liverpool in 2018. The Dutch centre-back holds the record for the most paid for a defender.

13 Neymar's name made headlines in 2014 when Barcelona (who bought him in 2013 from Santos) was charged with tax fraud for concealing the £71.5 million (€86.2 million) it had paid for him.

14 Chelsea broke the record for the biggest amount paid for a goalkeeper in 2018 when they picked up Kepa Arrizabalaga on a seven-year contract for £71.6 million (€80 million).

15 Widely regarded as one of the greatest footballers of all time, Zinedine Zidane held the world transfer record in 2001 when he moved from Juventus to Real Madrid for £46.6 million (€77.5 million).

16 Midfielder James Rodriguez also made the move there in 2014 for a reported £63 million (€76 million), making him the most expensive Colombian footballer.

17 When Alvaro Morata signed with Chelsea in 2017, he cost them £58 million (€65.5 million).

18 Midfielder Kevin De Bruyne crossed the Channel in 2015 to play for Manchester City. The British club paid £55 million (€75 million) for the Belgian.

19 The previous year fellow midfielder Ángel Di María had moved to City rival, Manchester United. The club paid £59.7 million (€75.6 million), the most paid by an English team at that time. A record now broken by Manchester United's fee for Paul Pogba.

20 Another big Manchester 2018 signing was Algeria's Riyad Mahrez. When City paid £60 million (€67.8 million) for him, he broke the record for an African player.

1. Marcos Bagdadis's tennis racquets took the brunt of his frustration at the 2012 Australian Open when he was losing to Stanislas Wawrinka. He broke four in a row, earning himself a $1,250 fine.
2. When England tied with Algeria 0–0 in the 2010 World Cup in South Africa, Wayne Rooney spoke directly to an on-pitch camera: 'Nice to see your home fans booing you,' he said angrily, 'That's what loyal support is.'
3. American sprinter John Drummond held up the 100-metre quarter-finals of the 2003 World Championships in Paris for 50 minutes when he lay on the track and refused to leave after being disqualified for a false start.
4. After South Korea's Ahn Jung-Hwan scored the winning goal that knocked Italy out of the World Cup in 2002, his contract with Italian club Perugia was swiftly terminated by Italian owner Luciano Gaucci.
5. When Russian gymnast Svetlana Khorkina lost out to American Carly Patterson in the women's all-round competition at the 2004 Olympic Games, she blamed the judges, claiming they discriminated against her nationality.
6. When Portugal lost 1–0 to Spain in the 2010 World Cup in Germany, Portuguese forward Cristiano Ronaldo was less than impressed and spat at a news cameraman who followed him off the pitch.
7. Swedish wrestler Ara Abrahamiam was so enraged about losing his semi-final match to Italy's Andrea Minguzzi at the 2008 Olympic Games that he had to be restrained from physically attacking the judges.
8. And he wasn't the only one – Cuban Taekwondo competitor Angel Matos used his martial arts skills on the referee, kicking him in the face, when he was disqualified from the bronze medal match. He received a lifetime ban.
9. US women's football goalkeeper Hope Solo suggested her former teammate Brandi Chastain get 'more educated' after the NBC analyst commented on her play during the 2012 Olympic Games.
10. Dutch speed skater Sjinkie Knegt lost the 5,000-metre race at the ISU European Short Track Championships to Russian Victor Ahn in 2014 and gave him two middle fingers as they crossed the finish line.

11. When Arsenal lost 2–1 to Tottenham in 2011, manager Arsène Wenger refused to shake hands with Tottenham assistant first team coach Clive Allen.

12. The same year, after an NFL game between the San Francisco 49ers and Detroit Lions, coaches Jim Harbaugh and Jim Schwartz shook hands. After a firm handshake and backslap, things soon got ugly and a brawl ensued.

13. Vancouver's city centre became a riot zone in 2011 when the Canucks ice hockey team lost to the Boston Bruins. On the night, 101 arrests were made and at least 4 people were stabbed.

14. In the quarter-final of the 2006 UK Championship, commentators and spectators were shocked when snooker player Ronnie O'Sullivan, having missed a pot, immediately called the game off and walked out conceding the 17-frame match after playing only 5 frames.

15. When defending champion Evgeni Plushenko came second to Evan Lysacek in the men's figure skating at the 2010 Winter Olympics, he told the media: 'I was positive I won, but I suppose Evan needs the medal more than I do.'

16. Serena Williams was widely criticised for calling umpire Carlos Ramos 'a thief' during the US Open final match against Naomi Osaka in 2018.

17. In 2009, LeBron James's Cleveland Cavaliers lost to Orlando Magic in the Eastern Conference Finals. The basketball star stormed off to the locker room refusing to take part in the customary players' handshake.

18. Arsenal captain William Gallas had a public tantrum in 2008 when his club lost vital league points in a 2–2 draw with Birmingham City. He kicked advertising hoardings and sulked in the middle of the pitch.

19. When racing driver Lewis Hamilton missed out on a victory at the 2018 British Grand Prix he was so angry he refused to be interviewed after the race, drawing widespread criticism.

20. When Canadian ice hockey coach Greg Holst was coaching Austrian team Villach, they lost to Vienna Capitals in 2006. After the game, he launched into an English–German rant, exclaiming: *'Es ist ein f*****g complete skandal!'* (It is a f*****g complete scandal).

20 INCREDIBLE SPORTING ACHIEVEMENTS

1. After the Rio de Janeiro Olympic Games, American swimmer Michael Phelps became the most decorated Olympian of all time, with a total of 28 medals, including 23 golds.
2. In 2017, American tennis player Serena Williams won her seventh Australian Open. It was her 23rd Grand Slam singles title, surpassing the record held by Steffi Graf.
3. When Swiss tennis star Roger Federer won the Australian Open in 2018, it was his 20th Grand Slam tournament win – the most for a male player. In 2019, he won his 100th ATP Tour title overall at the Dubai Tennis Championships, UAE – 6,600 days after winning his first in Milan, Spain.
4. British rower Steve Redgrave's victory at the 2000 Olympic Games in Sydney, Australia, made him the only athlete to win gold at five consecutive games in an endurance sport.
5. Lance Armstrong was the most successful Tour de France cyclist of all time before he was stripped of his medals in 2012 after the biggest doping scandal in cycling history. He had won the Tour seven times from 1999 to 2005.
6. Since Armstrong's fall from grace, British cyclist Chris Froome has become the twenty-first century's most victorious Tour de France winner, with four titles under his belt between 2013 and 2017.
7. New England Patriots quarterback Tom Brady became the only NFL player to be named the Super Bowl Most Valuable Player four times after he helped his team secure their fifth Super Bowl victory in 2017.
8. Between 2008 and 2017, football's prestigious Ballon d'Or was won five times each by Lionel Messi and Cristiano Ronaldo – meaning they hold jointly the record for most wins by any footballer in history.
9. In 2012, American basketball player LeBron James joined Michael Jordan as the only two players to win an NBA Most Valuable Player award, NBA championship, NBA Finals Most Valuable Player award and Olympic gold medal in the same year.
10. Ice hockey's Sidney Crosby joined only two other players in history when he won the Conn Smythe Trophy, Hart Memorial Trophy and World Cup Most Valuable Player award.

11. In 2008, Jamaican sprinter Usain Bolt became the first person to hold both world records for the 100 metres and 200 metres since fully automatic time became mandatory. In 2016, he became the only sprinter to win titles in those events at three consecutive Olympics.

12. British distance runner Mo Farah secured the 5,000- and 10,000-metre gold medals at two successive Olympic Games – the second athlete in modern history to do so since Lasse Virén in the 1970s.

13. On the track, Lewis Hamilton proved himself to be the most successful British and one of the greatest racing drivers in history, when in 2018 he secured his fifth Formula One title. He equalled Argentine driver Juan Manuel Fangio and is now only two wins away from Michael Schumacher's record of seven F1 titles.

14. Tiger Woods dominated golf in the 2000s, and in 2013 secured his 11th Professional Golfers' Association (PGA) Player of the Year title, five more than any other golfer before him.

15. American Olympian Simone Biles dominated the 2018 World Artistic Gymnastics Championships where she became the gymnast with the most gold medals of any gender.

16. In 2008, American racing driver Danika Patrick became the only woman to win an IndyCar Series race in Indy Japan 300.

17. Between 1996 and 2017, American boxer Floyd Mayweather fought and won 50 fights – 27 by knockouts and 23 by decisions.

18. In 2018, Shaun White secured a historic 100th US Olympic Winter Games gold medal. His win in the men's halfpipe event made him also the most gold-medal-decorated snowboarder of all time.

19. Norwegian cross-country skier Marit Bjørgen won five medals at the 2018 PyeongChang Winter Olympics, bringing her total Olympic medal haul to 15 – the most by any athlete, male or female.

20. After competing in both the 2003 and 2007 Rugby World Cups, England player Jonny Wilkinson became the tournament's biggest point scorer, with 277 points, and the only player to score points in two Rugby World Cup finals.

20 SENSATIONAL SPORTS STADIUMS

1. 2001 saw the Sapporo Dome open in Japan. Notable for its retractable grass soccer pitch that covers a baseball turf below, the stadium is truly multipurpose.
2. After London's Wembley Stadium was demolished in 2002, a new $1.3 billion replacement was built on the site. It has an iconic arch, measuring 133 metres (436 feet) high, over the stadium and 2,618 toilets (more than any other venue in the world).
3. In 2005, the Allianz Arena in Munich, Germany, opened. The new home of FC Bayern Munich has become one of Germany's most popular sporting venues. Its façade is made of nearly 3,000 Ethylene tetrafluoroethylene (ETFE) foil panels making it Europe's biggest stadium, with surrounding outdoor LED lighting for dynamic lighting moods. It can be illuminated red, blue or white, depending on which team is playing.
4. The Century Lotus Stadium in China's Guangdong province opened in 2006 at a cost of $155 million. It resembles a lotus flower and has an innovative spoked-wheel construction.
5. When the Emirates Stadium, London, was completed in 2006, it had cost Arsenal Football Club £390 million. But the new ground and facilities helped the club more than double its match-day revenue.
6. Known as the 'Bird's Nest', Beijing's National Stadium, China, was designed in collaboration with prominent Chinese artist Ai Weiwei and was completed in time for the Olympics in 2008.
7. Beijing is also home to China's National Aquatics Center, 'The Water Cube'. Overtaking the Bayern Munich stadium (Germany) record it was the world's biggest ETFE-shelled building when it opened in 2008.
8. The NFL's Dallas Cowboys home in Arlington, Texas, USA (the AT&T Stadium), was the largest domed structure in the world when it opened in 2009. It has a 105,000 capacity and is one of the most expensive stadiums ever built, costing $1.3 billion.
9. Cape Town Stadium, South Africa, completed in 2009, is nicknamed 'the Diva of Cape Town' and has a Teflon-coated fibreglass shell that responds to the city's weather, changing colour under different light conditions.
10. Opened in 2009, Taiwan's national Kaohsiung National Stadium harnesses solar energy for almost all its needs from 4,482 solar panels on the aluminium-framed plates that form the roof.

11. Beyoncé performed at the opening ceremony of Ukraine's Donbass Arena in Donetsk, winning the venue 'Event of the Year' at the 2010 Stadium Business Awards.
12. The First National Bank (FNB) Stadium in Johannesburg, South Africa, was redeveloped to host the 2010 FIFA World Cup Final. It was the place where, during the tournament's closing ceremony, Nelson Mandela made his last public appearance ever.
13. When New Jersey's MetLife Stadium, USA, opened in 2010, it took the crown for the most expensive stadium constructed ($1.6 billion).
14. Home to the Irish national rugby team and the Republic of Ireland's football team, the Aviva Stadium in Dublin opened in 2010. Because of its proximity to people's houses it has a façade and roof designed to let as much natural light through as possible.
15. China's Universiade Sports Center in Shenzen is named for the 2011 Summer Universiade, for which it was one of the venues. The global event for university athletes is the world's second largest multi-sport celebration in terms of participants.
16. Poland's Stadion Energa in Gdańsk was built as a host venue for the 2012 UEFA European Championship and can seat 42,000 people. Its façade is made from polycarbonate plates that look like amber – a mineral extracted in the Baltic Sea.
17. The Stadium at Queen Elizabeth Olympic Park, London, UK, was the host venue for the 2012 Summer Olympics. It was nominated for the Royal Institute of British Architects' Stirling Prize for Architecture.
18. Melbourne, Australia's AAMI Park was considered the world's most iconic stadium at the Stadium World Congress Awards 2012. Using 50 per cent less steel than equivalent structures, each of its 30,050 seats has an unobstructed view.
19. Also at the Stadium World Congress Awards 2012, Poland's National Stadium in Warsaw picked up the award for best multifunctional design. Its silver and red wire mesh façade is a nod to its national team's colours.
20. Millions tuned in to watch the opening ceremony of the 2014 Winter Olympics held at the Fisht Olympic Stadium in Sochi, Russia. It's named after Mount Fisht and was featured on a commemorative 100-ruble banknote. Reopened in 2016 as football stadium, it hosted matches as part of the 2017 FIFA Confederation Cup and 2018 FIFA World Cup.

20 SUPER BOWL HALF-TIME SHOWS

★ ★ ★ ★ ★ ★ ★ ★ ★ ★ ★ ★ ★ ★ ★ ★ ★ ★ ★ ★

1. 2000: At the Georgia Dome in Atlanta, the Disney-produced 'Tapestry of Nations' show was narrated by actor Edward James Olmos and included performances from Phil Collins and Tina Turner.

2. 2001: MTV's show in Tampa, Florida, saw Aerosmith and NSYNC playing a medley of both bands' songs. Their performance closed with everyone singing Aerosmith's 'Walk this Way'.

3. 2002: In the wake of the 9/11 attacks, Irish rock band U2 performed 'Where the Streets Have No Name' while names of the victims were projected onto a screen in the Louisiana Superdome, New Orleans.

4. 2003: San Diego's Qualcomm Stadium, California, was the setting for Shania Twain, No Doubt and Sting to perform at half-time.

5. 2004: Viewers complained after Justin Timberlake performed 'Rock Your Body' with Janet Jackson. At the end of the song, he accidentally pulled off part of her costume to expose her right breast.

6. 2005: Paul McCartney was considered a safe option the following year after the 2004 controversy. He played classic hits such as 'Hey Jude' and 'Drive My Car'.

7. 2006: When the Rolling Stones performed in Detroit, Michigan, the networks imposed a five-second broadcast delay and turned off Mick Jagger's microphone to avoid sexually explicit lyrics.

8. 2007: Prince was the headliner at the 41st Super Bowl half-time show, and the deluge of rain didn't stop him. If anything, the Miami, Florida, downpour enhanced his closing number: 'Purple Rain'.

9. 2008: The Emmy-nominated show featured Tom Petty and the Heartbreakers singing 'American Girl' and 'Free Fallin'', among other hits.

10. 2009: Bruce Springsteen had been asked to perform at the Super Bowl before, and finally agreed this year. To fit in the 12-minute time slot, Springsteen dropped verses from all of his four songs.

11. 2010: When The Who performed a medley of their hits, it was the first time in a decade that a crowd of fans hadn't surrounded the stage for the performance.

⑫ 2011: Usher and Slash accompanied The Black Eyed Peas on stage at Cowboys Stadium in Arlington, Texas.

⑬ 2012: Before being overtaken in 2015, Madonna's highly anticipated performance was the most-viewed half-time show ever, smashing a record set by Michael Jackson in 1993.

⑭ 2013: Beyoncé's spectacular show featured a reunion with former Destiny's Child bandmates – and was a possible cause of a power blackout in the stadium in the game's third quarter.

⑮ 2014: New Jersey welcomed Bruno Mars and special guests the Red Hot Chili Peppers to the stage. The latter received criticism for faking their instrumental performance (their guitars were not connected on stage).

⑯ 2015: Katy Perry broke Madonna's most-watched Super Bowl half-time show record. Her performance was seen by 118.5 million television viewers. She entered the stage atop a giant gold mechanical lion singing 'Roar'.

⑰ 2016: The fiftieth Super Bowl was headlined by Coldplay, and featured Beyoncé performing her new single 'Formation' with back-up dancers dressed as Black Panthers.

⑱ 2017: Lady Gaga performed solo but was accompanied by a fleet of 300 LED-equipped drones that were synchronised to form an image of the American flag behind her on stage.

⑲ 2018: Justin Timberlake was invited back for his third half-time performance – 14 years after 'boob-gate'. The show was notable for its avoidance of pyrotechnics, using lasers and video screens instead.

⑳ 2019: After SpongeBob SquarePants creator Stephen Hillenburg died in late 2018, fans petitioned for a marching band song from the cartoon to be performed at the Super Bowl. It was headlined by American pop group Maroon 5, who paid tribute to SpongeBob SquarePants with a clip of 'Sweet Victory', a song that the cast of SpongeBob SquarePants performed in an episode from 2001.

20 CHANGES TO **THE OLYMPIC GAMES**

1. The Sydney, Australia, Games in 2000 were the first to feature two new Olympic sports: taekwondo and triathlon. The triathlon included a 1,500-metre open-water swim.

2. 2002 saw a brand new sport for the Winter Olympics in Salt Lake City, USA – skeleton.

3. At the 2004 Games in Greece, a maximum quota of 136 was put on the number of athletes allowed in the diving competition. Quotas were reduced in boxing, canoe-kayak, equestrian and judo.

4. In 2005, baseball and softball were dropped from the Summer Olympics. They were last included in the 2008 Games but did not feature in London in 2012…

5. … That reduced the total number of sports for the 2012 Summer Olympics from 28 to 26, the lowest number of sports since Atlanta, USA, in 1996.

6. Open-water swimming rose to prominence in 2008 when a race of 10 kilometres (6.2 miles) was part of the Beijing Olympics in China.

7. BMX racing appeared for the first time in 2008. The 2020 games will feature BMX freestyle events for the first time.

8. Women's boxing was added as an Olympic sport in 2012, with women competing in 3 out of 13 weight classes.

9. Women ski jumpers had to wait until 2014 to compete in the Olympic Games. Despite filing a lawsuit against the Organizing Committee of the 2010 Winter Olympics in Vancouver, Canada, citing a violation under the Canadian Charter of Rights and Freedoms, they were not included in these Games.

10. In 2009, the International Olympic Committee (IOC) voted to include golf and rugby sevens in the 2016 Summer Olympics. Both had been Olympic sports before, rugby sevens from 1900 to 1924 and golf from 1900 to 1908.

⓫ 2012 was the first year that women competed in every sport included in the Olympic programme. It was also the first year every country was represented by both male and female athletes.

⓬ London 2012 featured mixed doubles tennis for the first time, as well as men and women both competing in the same five track cycling events: sprint, team sprint, keirin, team pursuit and omnium.

⓭ In 2013, the IOC decided to reduce the number of sports for the 2020 line-up. Although modern pentathlon, taekwondo and wrestling were considered, it was wrestling that was eventually dropped.

⓮ Later in 2013, after an outcry, wrestling was voted back in over baseball, softball and squash.

⓯ In 2015, the International Gymnastics Federation voted to reduce the Olympic team size from five to four gymnasts for the 2020 Games.

⓰ In 2016, the IOC added baseball/softball, karate, sport climbing, surfing and skateboarding to the roster for the 2020 Summer Olympics.

⓱ At the 2016 Games in Rio de Janeiro, kitesurfing made its Olympic debut, replacing windsurfing in the programme of events.

⓲ In 2014, ice climbing featured as a demonstration sport at the Winter Olympics, the first new sport to be showcased in this way since 1992. The aim is that it should become an official sport at the 2022 Games.

⓳ In 2016, Kosovo and South Sudan took part for the first time. There was also a team made up of refugee athletes from four countries who could not compete under their home nation.

⓴ The Tokyo Games in 2020 will be the first Olympics to have a total of 33 sports, the most of any modern Olympic Games.

20 MEMORABLE OSCAR SPEECHES

1. When Angelina Jolie won the Best Supporting Actress Oscar in 2000 for her role in *Girl Interrupted*, she sparked incest rumours by declaring her love for her brother and locking lips with him on the red carpet.

2. Julia Roberts wasn't going to let her 2001 Best Actress Oscar win for *Erin Brockovich* pass her by. 'You're so quick with that stick', she said to the conductor trying to play her out, 'so why don't you sit'.

3. In 2002, Halle Berry became the first black woman to receive a Best Actress Oscar for *Monster's Ball*. She declared the award was for 'every nameless, faceless woman of colour that now has a chance because this door has been opened'.

4. When Adrien Brody came up onto the stage in 2003 to receive the Best Actor Oscar for *The Pianist*, he preceded his speech by pulling presenter Halle Berry into a full-on smooch.

5. There were lots of awkward pauses in 2004 when Sean Penn won Best Actor for *Mystic River*. He hadn't written a speech, and it showed.

6. Michael Moore was booed off stage after calling out President George W. Bush for the Iraq War in his acceptance speech for receiving the Best Documentary Oscar for *Bowling for Columbine* in 2003.

7. Heath Ledger died tragically in 2008. In the 2009 Oscar ceremony he was awarded a posthumous Academy Award for Best Supporting Actor for his role as the Joker in the Batman film, *The Dark Knight*. His grieving family – including mother, Sally Bell, father, Kim Ledger, and sister, Kate – accepted the award on his behalf.

8. *Milk* screenwriter Dustin Lance Black used his Oscar-winning moment in 2009 to highlight the ongoing struggle of the LGBTQ community. Telling young gay and lesbian kids, 'I promise you, you will have equal rights.'

9. Rodger Ross Williams's 2010 acceptance speech for directing the short documentary *Music by Prudence* (the first African-American to win this award) was awkwardly interrupted by the film's other producer Elinor Burkett.

10. It was an emotional moment in 2010 when Kathryn Bigelow became the first woman to win a Best Director Oscar for *The Hurt Locker*, beating four men, including her ex-husband James Cameron.

11. After taking out shameless adverts in the Hollywood trade press on a personal Oscar campaign, Melissa Leo dropped the F-bomb during her Best Supporting Actress speech for *The Fighter* in 2011.

12. Meryl Streep has been nominated for acting Oscars 21 times. Her last win came in 2012 for *The Iron Lady* when she made a joke that she could hear half of America exclaiming, 'Oh no! Her, again!'

13. Jennifer Lawrence took the 'trip of a lifetime' when she fell on the stairs after winning Best Actress for *Silver Linings Playbook* in 2013. The trip got a mention in the speech.

14. While it wasn't an acceptance speech, the talk of the 2014 Oscars was how John Travolta introduced Broadway star Idina Menzel as 'Adele Dazeem'.

15. When Patricia Arquette won the Best Supporting Actress award for *Boyhood* in 2015, she used her platform to call out the gender pay gap, to rapturous applause from the likes of Meryl Streep and Jennifer Lopez.

16. When singer John Legend and rapper Common picked up the award for Best Song in 2015 for 'Glory' from the film *Selma*, they drew attention to voting rights and the incarceration of black men.

17. It was sixth time's a charm for Leonardo DiCaprio when he finally won an Oscar for *The Revenant* in 2016. His speech focused on an issue close to his heart – climate change.

18. The most talked about Oscar speech in 2017 was when *La La Land*'s producers started accepting the award for Best Picture, before the announcers' mistake was rather cringingly rectified. *Moonlight* had actually won.

19. Frances McDormand invited all female nominees to stand in the theatre with her as she gave her acceptance speech for Best Actress in 2018 for *Three Billboards Outside Ebbing, Missouri*, highlighting the importance of female talent.

20. When Mark Bridges won Best Costume Design for *Phantom Thread* in 2018, his 30-second speech won him a jet ski, which host Jimmy Kimmel had promised for the shortest acceptance speech.

20 ARTWORKS THAT SOLD AT AUCTION

1. In 2001, after the discovery that Peter Paul Rubens's *Massacre of the Innocents* had been miscategorised as the work of one of his assistants in the eighteenth century, it sold for $76.7 million.
2. Five years after buying London-based Chelsea Football Club in 2003, Russian billionaire Roman Abramovich splashed $86.3 million on Francis Bacon's *Triptych.*
3. Sotheby's auction house made a tidy commission of $11 million when they sold Pablo Picasso's *Garcon a la pipe* in 2004 for $104 million.
4. *No. 5, 1948* by American painter Jackson Pollock was originally owned by Samuel Irving Newhouse and displayed at New York's Museum of Modern Art (MoMA). In 2006 it sold at auction for $140 million.
5. In 2006, *Woman III* by abstract expressionist Willem de Kooning sold to billionaire Steven A. Cohen for $137.5 million, making it the second most expensive painting ever sold.
6. *Portrait of Adele Bloch-Bauer I* took Gustav Klimt 3 years to paint. In 2006, 99 years after its completion, it was bought by Ronald Lauder for $135 million.
7. Its sister painting, *Portrait of Adele Bloch-Bauer II*, was also sold in 2006 for the slightly more affordable $88 million. Adele Block-Bauer was the only model painted twice by Klimt.
8. Picasso hit the news again in 2006 when his *Dora Maar au Chat*, a 1941 work depicting the artist's lover with a cat on her shoulders, sold for $83.4 million.
9. And then Picasso's *Nude, Green Leaves and Bust* broke records when it went for $106.5 million in 2010. It had previously been in the private collection of Sidney and Frances Brody for nearly 60 years.
10. When the Andy Warhol painting *Eight Elvises*, which was 3.7 metres (12 feet) tall, was sold in 2008 for $100 million, this price became the most paid for a work by the prolific artist.

11. The 2008 sale of Damien Hirst's *The Golden Calf* for $18.5 million was part of a record-breaking two-day sale. The Sotheby's event made more than $198 million, the most made at an auction dedicated to a single artist.

12. In 2008, *Keep It Spotless* by Banksy sold in a charity auction of the artist's work for $1.7 million. The spray-painted work depicts a Los Angeles (USA) hotel maid appearing to sweep under the painting.

13. Bainbridges auction house in London was the setting for the 2010 sale of an eighteenth-century Qianlong dynasty vase. It sold for $85.9 million.

14. A record $105.2 million was paid for Alberto Giacometti's bronze cast sculpture *L'homme qui Marche I* in 2010. The 1961 artwork, literally translated as 'The Walking Man' was initially created for, but never displayed at, the Chase Manhattan Plaza in New York.

15. Five years later, another bronze sculpture, Giacometti's *L'homme au doigt* comfortably broke the artist's record when it sold for $141.3 million to a private buyer.

16. There are four versions of Edvard Munch's painting *The Scream*, but only one is privately owned. In 2012, it went on sale and fetched $119.9 million.

17. 2013 saw Jeff Koons' *Balloon Dog* become the most expensive piece of art by a living artist when it made $58.4 million at auction.

18. Amedeo Modigliani's iconic *Nu couché* was sold at Christie's in New York in 2015 for a record $170.4 million (the most ever paid for a work by the artist). It was reportedly bought by Liu Yiqian using an American Express card.

19. Competing Norman Rockwell fans pushed up the price of his painting *Saying Grace* in 2017 – it finally sold for $46 million (it was estimated to go for $15–$20 million).

20. When you factor in the auction house's premium, Leonardo da Vinci's *Salvator Mundi* shattered all previous sales records when it went for $450.3 million at Christie's in 2017.

20 SONGS THAT GOT STUCK IN YOUR HEAD

1. Widely thought of as Kylie Minogue's signature song, 'I Can't Get You Out of My Head' was released in 2001 and reached number one in 40 countries.

2. 2001's Grammy Song of the Year was U2's 'Beautiful Day'. It was a huge commercial success for the band and they have played it at every concert in the years since.

3. In 2017, *Billboard* magazine named 'Lose Yourself' Eminem's best song. The 2002 song from the film *8 Mile* stayed at number one in the United States for 12 weeks in a row. It was also the first rap song to win an Oscar.

4. VH1 declared Beyoncé's 2003 hit 'Crazy in Love' to be the song of the 2000s. It was the lead single from her first solo album and featured her future husband Jay-Z.

5. The White Stripes released 'Seven Nation Army' in 2003. The song's recognisable riff made it an instant classic – it won the Grammy for Best Rock Song in 2004.

6. 'Mr Brightside' was the first single released by American rock band The Killers. The 2004 hit is about a man who suspects his partner is cheating on him.

7. Britney Spears received her first Grammy Award in 2005 for Best Dance Recording for catchy pop hit 'Toxic'. Britney later revealed it's her favourite of all her dance songs.

8. Many parents across the world have come to fear the words 'Baby Shark'. Although it is said to have originated earlier, 2015 saw the painfully catchy tune go viral thanks to a delightful video produced by kids' entertainment company Pinkfong.

9. Amy Winehouse's hugely popular 'Rehab' was released in 2006 and went on to win three Grammy Awards at the 50th ceremony and an Ivor Novello Award.

10. In 2007, Rihanna's 'Umbrella' was one of the biggest-selling singles of the year. The British press jokingly blamed the track for the extreme rainfall and flooding that occurred after its release.

11. 'Poker Face' by Lady Gaga came out in 2009 and became the biggest-selling single of the year worldwide by digital downloads.

12. British singer-songwriter Adele was catapulted to international fame after she released 'Rolling in the Deep' in 2010. It was her first number one single in the United States.

13. 'In Da Club' by rapper 50 Cent ranked 13th in *Rolling Stone* magazine's 2010 best songs of the decade. It broke a *Billboard* magazine record in 2003 for the most listened to song in radio history.

14. Carly Rae Jepson's 'Call Me Maybe' was the bestselling single worldwide in 2012. It was also named MTV's Song of the Year.

15. In 2012, the music video for Psy's 'Gangnam Style' became the first to receive one billion views. The accompanying dance moves became a pop culture sensation.

16. The video for 2014 song 'Uptown Funk' is one of the most viewed uploads on YouTube. The Mark Ronson song features Bruno Mars.

17. Justin Bieber's 2015 catchy release 'Sorry' became one of the bestselling digital music releases, with over 10 million downloads in 2016 alone.

18. 'Happy' by Pharrell Williams was featured on the *Despicable Me 2* film's soundtrack. It was the biggest-selling single of 2014 by digital downloads.

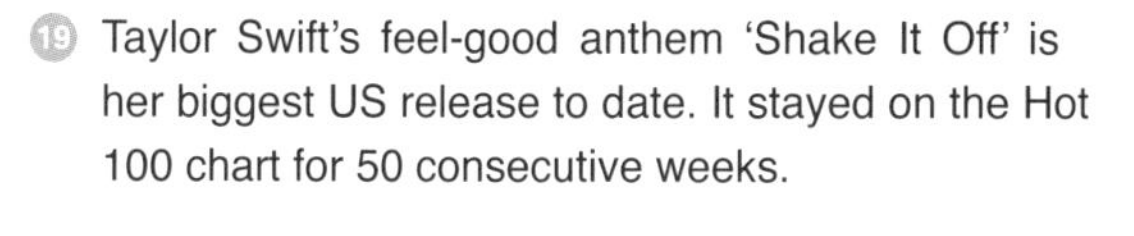

19. Taylor Swift's feel-good anthem 'Shake It Off' is her biggest US release to date. It stayed on the Hot 100 chart for 50 consecutive weeks.

20. While some criticised it as a novelty song, there was no denying the popularity of Meghan Trainor's 2014 anthem 'All About That Bass' – it topped the charts in 21 countries.

20 TV FINALES

1. 'The Last One' was the title of the *Friends* finale, which aired in 2004, bringing to a close one of the most successful sitcoms of all time.

2. Fans were left divided over the final episode of *Lost* in 2010. After years of questions about the true nature of 'the island', there were few answers to be found.

3. *The Sopranos*' finale 'Made in America', which aired in 2007, is one of the most hotly discussed in TV history and left the audience wondering if mafioso Tony Soprano was dead or not.

4. The 2005 finale of family mortician drama *Six Feet Under* included a montage that showed how all the key characters ended up dying.

5. *Breaking Bad* was one of the most-watched cable shows on American television when the finale aired in 2013. The episode hurtled towards a dramatic end for both the lead characters, when Walt died.

6. After years of searching, *Battlestar Galactica*'s Cylon robots finally found a planet to call home in the 2009 series finale.

7. Corrupt-cop drama *The Shield* finished anti-hero style in 2008 after seven seasons with the lead police character working a desk job.

8. In 2014, the ninth season of CBS's *How I Met Your Mother* finally revealed the identity of 'the mother' and saw how the key characters' lives turn out in the future.

9. In the UK, the *Buffy the Vampire Slayer* finale, which aired in 2003, was the show's highest-rated episode ever.

10. In the same year, teenage drama *Dawson's Creek* ended with a five-year flash-forward episode that finally saw Dawson becoming a successful film director.

11. *Mad Men* was a TV series about the advertising industry in the 1960s. The final scene of the critically acclaimed programme ended with the iconic 'I Want to Buy the World a Coke' commercial, and Don Draper's fate unknown.

12. *The Office* (British version) may have only lasted for two series, but the ending of the final episode was heart-breaking for viewers in 2002. Thank goodness the Christmas Specials gave Tim and Dawn a happy ending a year later.

13. The American series of *The Office* by comparison lasted for nine seasons, bowing out only in 2013, despite lead actor Steve Carrell having left the show two seasons previously.

14. Carrie Bradshaw finally got her happy ending in *Sex and the City*'s final episode in 2004 (although it wasn't the last viewers would see of her thanks to two movies that followed).

15. Millions of British viewers tuned in to watch the eagerly anticipated finale of time-travelling police series *Life on Mars*, which finished after 16 episodes in 2007.

16. Widely referred to as one of the worst endings, *Dexter*'s final moments of season eight revealed that the vigilante serial killer was still alive and living as a lumberjack in Oregon.

17. Political satire television sitcom *Parks and Recreation* was one of the biggest comedy series of the 2010s. It ended in a suitably silly fashion in 2015 with a flash-forward episode that ended in 2048 hinting that Leslie might be President of the United States.

18. *The Good Wife* was an award-winning legal drama series that ran for seven seasons. Its finale aired in 2016 and saw the complex central character of Alicia Florrick left single and without a job after choosing to stand by her husband for the last time.

19. The season eight finale of *24* aired in 2010 and followed the 24-hour timeframe the show was known for with an hour of action passing in each episode. The show was revived in 2014.

20. *CSI: Crime Scene Investigation* ran between 2000 and 2015. After 337 episodes the show ended with a feature-length finale called 'Immortality'.

20 MODERN ART MOMENTS

1. After serving as President of the United States, George W. Bush took up painting as a hobby. In 2013 his sister's email was hacked and photos of the paintings, including some self-portraits of him bathing, appeared online.

2. First performed in 1995, Oscar-winning actress Tilda Swinton chose New York's Museum of Modern Art (MoMA), to return to *The Maybe* in 2013, a performative artwork that saw the actress sleep in a glass box in the gallery.

3. American actor Shia LaBeouf turned his back on his frivolous celebrity life and became a performance artist, most notably with his 2015 work, *All My Movies* in which he watched his cinematic back catalogue with members of the public.

4. Damien Hirst's diamond skull sculpture *For the Love of God* went on display in 2007. It was made from an eighteenth-century skull encrusted with nearly 9,000 diamonds, costing him more than £14 million to produce.

5. Street artist Banksy made the headlines in 2015 when he erected a temporary artwork in the British seaside town of Weston-super-Mare, Somerset, UK. *Dismaland* was a sinister twist on Disneyland.

6. Shepard Fairey's *Hope* posters, featuring presidential candidate Barack Obama, became one of the most iconic images of the 2008 American presidential campaign.

7. In 2011, Chinese artist Ai Weiwei disappeared for 81 days after being detained by authorities. He was eventually released on bail, without his passport, and issued with a huge tax bill.

8. In 2012, people queued for up to 12 hours in London to experience *Rain Room*, an installation artwork by collective Random International that used motion detectors to create a dry path for visitors to walk through a room of falling water.

9. Japanese artist Yayoi Kusama's work *Infinity Mirrored Room – Filled with the Brilliance of Life* at the Tate Modern, London, was an arresting installation composed of hundreds of LED lights, shifting colours and reflections by mirrors.

10. A Marina Abramović retrospective was held at MoMA in 2010, at which she also performed *The Artist is Present.* The artwork saw Abramović sit in silence for over 736 hours in the museum's atrium while spectators sat opposite her.

11. In 2006, Mexican artist Pablo Helguera took a travelling schoolhouse across the Americas as part of *The School of Panamerican Unrest* to create a forum for debate about immigration, globalisation and art.

12. In 2014, the defunct Domino Sugar Factory in Brooklyn, New York, was taken over by a collection of sugar-made and sugar-coated sculptures. *A Subtlety* by Kara Walker was dominated by a huge sphinx-like figure of a woman with African features.

13. Argentinian artist Marta Minujín's *The Parthenon of Forbidden Books* took over a park in Kassel, Germany, that had been a Nazi book-burning site in 1933. The classic Greek temple was recreated in 2017 using 10,000 prohibited books.

14. When the US government overturned an Obama-era executive order allowing transgender people to use the public bathrooms that correspond with their gender identity, Canadian artist Cassils collected their urine for 200 days and displayed it in a Plexiglass cube.

15. In 2011, *The Birth of Baby X* saw Marni Kotak, a New York-based performance artist, give birth to her son as the culmination of her performance.

16. In 2003, the Tate Gallery's Turbine Hall in London was filled by Olafur Eliasson's *The Weather Project* – a semi-circle of light reflected in a mirror to create the illusion of a burning sun.

17. At Art Cologne, Germany, 2014, Swiss-born performance artist Milo Moire created abstract paintings by pushing ink- and paint-filled eggs out of her vaginal canal while standing naked above a canvas.

18. Artist Adrian Parsons, known for his political performance art, went on a 25-day hunger strike (2012) and lived in an art gallery for 48 hours (2013), but his most controversial performance occurred in 2007, when he decided to perform his own circumcision of himself on stage.

19. In 2012, Russian punk band Pussy Riot broke into the Moscow Cathedral of Christ the Saviour, Russia, to perform a 'punk prayer' from the altar, a criticism of the church's ties to President Vladimir Putin. Six members were charged with crimes in relation to the performance.

20. In 2011, Brooklyn-based artist Kyle McDonald installed software on an Apple Store's computer that took photos of customers' expressionless faces as they stared at computer screens.

20 plays that got people talking

❶ In 2018, when *Harry Potter and The Cursed Child* opened in New York, it made Broadway history as the bestselling show in one week. It took $2.28 million from eight shows.

❷ *The Lion King* might not be New York's longest-running musical, but in 2013, after 16 years, it became the first Broadway show to gross $1 billion dollars.

❸ In 2014, Norm Lewis made history when he became the first African-American actor to perform the role of the Phantom in *The Phantom of the Opera* on Broadway, New York.

❹ Opening in 2011 in New York, *The Book of Mormon* was a huge hit, with the album recorded by its cast becoming the highest-charting Broadway album (at number 3) in 40 years.

❺ When *Spider-Man: Turn Off the Dark* opened in 2011 in New York, it was famous for technical difficulties, cast injuries and having the most preview nights in Broadway history (182 performances).

❻ Among its many accolades, Lin-Manuel Miranda's *Hamilton* won the Pulitzer Prize for Drama in 2016, only the ninth musical to do so since the award was started almost 100 years earlier.

❼ In 2007, West End theatre sales soared in London when 17-year-old Harry Potter star Daniel Radcliffe trod the boards in *Equus*. The part required the young actor to be naked on stage.

❽ In London, *Viva Forever!*, staged in 2012, was one of the West End's most widely criticised shows. The show featured the Spice Girls' music and was written by Jennifer Saunders.

❾ Launching the careers of James Corden, Dominic Cooper and Russell Tovey, *The History Boys* opened in 2004 at London's Royal National Theatre. The cast went on to star in a film of the same name.

10. One of the most widely anticipated shows of 2007 was *Lord of the Rings*, and it was the most expensive West End show of all time when it opened in London, costing £25 million.

11. *Billy Elliot*, the musical version of the popular film, with music by Elton John, became a West End staple in 2005. It spent 11 years at the Victoria Palace Theatre, London.

12. When tickets were released for London's Barbican production of *Hamlet* starring Benedict Cumberbatch in 2015, it became the fastest-selling production in British history. Fans camped for 17 hours to try and pick up the few tickets available each day.

13. The National Theatre, London, transformed the book *War Horse* by Michael Morpurgo into a theatrical masterpiece complete with life-size horse puppets.

14. In 2015, a British man fainted during a West End, London, production of *Dry Land*. The play includes a scene where a teenage girl takes an abortion pill, prompting her to miscarry.

15. In London, Australian actress Nicole Kidman was widely praised for her 2015 performance in *Photograph 51* in which she played X-ray crystallographer Rosalind Franklin.

16. Between 2013 and 2015, Hollywood stars Michelle Williams, Emma Stone and Sienna Miller all stepped into the Broadway, New York, role of Sally Bowles in *Cabaret*.

17. In 2015, a student climbed onto the stage before the curtain rose on a performance of *Hand to God* on Broadway, New York, to try to charge his mobile phone from a non-functioning power socket.

18. Kathleen Turner and Jerry Hall both bared all when they took on the role of Mrs Robinson in the stage adaptation of *The Graduate* in the early 2000s.

19. In 2016, when Sarah Kane's play *Cleansed* was staged for the second time at the National Theatre in London, there were reports of various people storming out and fainting because of the play's graphic torture scenes.

20. In 2005, when *Mercury Fur* premiered in Plymouth, Devon, it became a theatrical sensation for the high number of walkouts each night. Publishers Faber & Faber even refused to publish Philip Ridley's script, which involves the murder of a child.

20 RECORD-BREAKING MOVIES

1. 2018's Marvel superhero film *Avengers: Infinity War* was the film with the biggest worldwide opening weekend on record, taking over $640 million.

2. James Cameron's *Avatar*, which came out in 2009, is one of the highest-grossing films of all time at the time of writing, with theatrical release earnings of over $2.8 billion.

3. Adjusted for inflation, 2017's remake of Stephen King's *It* became the highest-grossing horror film of all time, making over $700 million at the box office.

4. 2013's *Frozen* wowed audiences with its female-centric cast and catchy soundtrack. It's the highest-grossing animated film of all time, making over $1.2 billion at the box office.

5. But when it comes to stop-motion animation, nothing has yet been able to surpass 2000's *Chicken Run*. In the years since, it has made a whopping $224 million.

6. Live-action musicals have also broken records, with 2017's *Beauty and the Beast*, *The Greatest Showman* and 2016's *La La Land* all making it into the top five highest-grossing musical films of all time.

7. The title for worst opening weekend for a film shown on 3,000 cinema screens or more goes to 2006's *Hoot*, a story about children protecting an owl habitat starring Luke Wilson. It made just over $3 million and cost $15 million to make.

8. The highest-grossing non-English-speaking film was *Wolf Warrior 2* in 2017, a Chinese action film directed by Wu Gang. In China, it had the biggest single-day gross.

9. And not far behind, it's followed closely by Chinese sci-fi film *The Wandering Earth* (2019, $684 million) and 2004's *The Passion of the Christ*. The Mel Gibson-helmed project is largely in Aramaic, Latin and Hebrew, which had a worldwide gross of $612 million.

10. The latter is also the highest-grossing R-rated film in US history, although a number of films have vied for the title in recent years, including *Deadpool*, *American Sniper* and *It*.

11. 2019 was a landmark year for streaming service and production company, Netflix. Their film *Roma* won Best Picture at the British Academy of Film and Television Arts (BAFTA) Awards and scored three Oscars for Best Director, Best Cinematography and Best Foreign Language Film.

12. The three top-grossing films of 2017, *Star Wars: The Last Jedi*, *Beauty and the Beast* and *Wonder Woman* all had female leads. It had been nearly 60 years since female-led films had taken the top three spots.

13. In 2017, *La La Land* joined *All About Eve* and *Titanic* for having the most Oscar nominations in cinematic history, with 14 nods, although it only won six.

14. In 2003, *The Lord of the Rings: The Return of the King*, the third in the trilogy, won all the eleven awards it was nominated for – tying with *Ben Hur* and *Titanic* for the record of the most Academy awards won by a single film.

15. With a production budget of just $15,000, the 2007 horror film *Paranormal Activity* became one of the most profitable films of all time, with worldwide takings of over $193 million.

16. The highest-grossing Bollywood film of all time opened in December 2016. *Dangal*, which was co-produced by Walt Disney Studios, was also the fifth highest-grossing non-English-language film of all time.

17. When Ron Howard's *The Da Vinci Code* came out in 2006, it became the most-banned film in the last 20 years. Censors in China, Egypt, Jordan, Lebanon, Pakistan, the Philippines, Samoa and the Solomon Islands refused to release it.

18. The highest-grossing IMAX film is the 2002-released *Space Station 3-D*, a documentary about life on the International Space Station narrated by Tom Cruise. It was also the first IMAX 3D film produced in space.

19. Recent winners of the Golden Raspberry Awards in recognition of the year's worst movies, have included *The Last Airbender*, *Transformers: Revenge of the Fallen*, *The Emoji Movie* and *Fifty Shades of Grey*.

20. At the time of writing, several twenty-first-century films have a 100 per cent Rotten Tomatoes score. Among them are *Man on Wire* (2008), *Mr. Roosevelt* (2017), *Paddington 2* (2018) and *Leave No Trace* (2018).

20 Authors, Playwrights, Poets and Musicians Who Won a Pulitzer Prize

1. Michael Chabon's *The Amazing Adventures of Kavalier & Clay* picked up the Pulitzer Prize for Fiction in 2001. The story centres around two boy geniuses who become major players in the comic book industry in wartime New York.

2. *Proof* by David Auburn was the play that won the 2001 Pulitzer Prize for Drama and the Tony Award for Best Play.

3. In 2003, Jeffrey Eugenides was awarded the Pulitzer Prize for Fiction for his book *Middlesex*, a novel about a Greek-American intersex person who is genetically a boy but is raised as a girl.

4. *On the Transmigration of Souls* was a musical commemoration for the victims of the 9/11 attacks. It premiered a year after the tragedy and was awarded the Pulitzer Prize for Music in 2003.

5. *Doubt: A Parable*, written by John Patrick Shanley, picked up the Pulitzer Prize for Drama in 2005. Shortly after, it was made into a film starring Meryl Streep, Philip Seymour Hoffman, Amy Adams and Viola Davis in Oscar-nominated roles.

6. Claudia Emerson's collection of poetry *Late Wife*, in which a woman addresses her former husband, new husband and herself, won the 2006 Pulitzer Prize for Poetry. Emerson died aged 57 from colon cancer in 2014.

7. 2007's *The Looming Tower* by Lawrence Wright was a sweeping non-fiction narrative about the events leading up to 9/11. He spent five years researching to write it and interviewed hundreds of people. It picked up the Pulitzer Prize for General Non-Fiction.

8. Cormac McCarthy's *The Road* was the Pulitzer Prize for Fiction winner in 2007 and was selected for Oprah Winfrey's Book Club the same year. The novel was dedicated to the author's son, whom he later insisted was a co-author of the book.

9. The Pulitzer Prize for Music in 2007 went to Ornette Coleman for *Sound Grammar*. The live jazz album was the saxophonist and composer's first new album in almost ten years.

10. *August: Osage County* was the Pulitzer Prize for Drama winner in 2008. The play is a family-centred comedy-drama that takes place over several weeks in Oklahoma, USA.

11. Many of the stories that make up *A Visit from the Goon Squad* by Jennifer Egan, the 2011 Pulitzer Prize for Fiction winner, appeared first as short stories in magazines.

12. Siddhartha Mukherjee's 2011 *The Emperor of All Maladies: A Biography of Cancer* charted the disease's 5,000-year lifespan and earned him a Pulitzer Prize for General Non-Fiction.

13. In 2012, Tracy K. Smith received the Pulitzer Prize for Poetry for her collection *Life on Mars*. In 2017 she became the 22nd Poet Laureate of the United States.

14. Donna Tartt spent 11 years working on her 784-page *The Goldfinch*, which starts with the theft of the Carel Fabritius painting of the same name. In 2014 it won the Pulitzer Prize for Fiction.

15. Despite not being set in America, as many Pulitzer Prize-winning fiction books are, Anthony Doerr's World War Two masterpiece, *All the Light We Cannot See* was worthy of the 2015 honour.

16. The Pulitzer Prize for General Non-Fiction winner that year was Elizabeth Colbert. The *New Yorker* staff writer's book, *The Sixth Extinction: An Unnatural History*, explored the threat posed by human behaviour on our planet.

17. In 2016, the landmark American musical *Hamilton*, written by Lin-Manuel Miranda, took home the Pulitzer Prize for Drama. It has become one of the most successful Broadway shows of all time.

18. Colson Whitehead won the 2017 Pulitzer Prize for Fiction for his bestselling slavery-era novel *The Underground Railroad*.

19. James Forman Jr's 2018 General Non-Fiction-winning book *Locking Up Our Own: Crime and Punishment in Black America* was an examination of the historical roots of the country's criminal justice system.

20. American rapper Kendrick Lamar's 2018 album *DAMN.* became the first non-jazz or classical work to receive the Pulitzer Prize for Music.

20 Books that People Couldn't Put Down

1. Stephanie Meyer was the bestselling author of 2008 and 2009 in America, where her four-book vampire series *Twilight* dominated the charts.

2. *The Girl with the Dragon Tattoo* was the first book in the *Millennium* series by Swedish author Stieg Larsson. The book was published after his death in 2004 and was adapted into a successful film franchise.

3. One of the biggest books of 2012 for its 'he said/she said' suspenseful plot was Gillian Flynn's *Gone Girl*. It sold over two million copies in its first year of publication and was made into an Oscar-nominated 2014 David Fincher film, for which Flynn produced the screenplay.

4. 2007 was the year the final book in the Harry Potter phenomenon, *Harry Potter and the Deathly Hallows*, hit bookshops. The book was launched at London's Natural History Museum with author J. K. Rowling and 1,700 lucky guests.

5. Young adult fiction saw a surge in popularity, particularly with Suzanne Collins' *The Hunger Games* series, which was translated into 51 languages.

6. When HBO premiered *Game of Thrones* in 2011, it was the same year George R. R. Martin released the fifth book in his epic fantasy series, *A Song of Ice and Fire*, which the TV series was based on. Readers have been waiting eight years for the sixth book.

7. Jeff Kinney's *Diary of a Wimpy Kid* series has dominated Young Readers' bestseller lists since the first book came out in 2007, with over 200 million books sold so far.

8. 2006 memoir *Eat, Pray, Love*, about Elizabeth Gilbert's travels in Italy, India and Indonesia, remained in *The New York Times*' bestseller list for over 200 weeks.

9. When *The Da Vinci Code* came out in 2003, it was initially outsold by the fifth Harry Potter book. But Dan Brown's mystery thriller has gone on to sell more than 80 million copies, making it the bestselling book published in the twenty-first century, still no match though for all-time leader *Don Quixote*'s 500 million copies.

10. After Oprah Winfrey invited Rhonda Byrne, author of *The Secret*, to appear on her show in January 2017, the book's 'power of positive thinking' message reached the mainstream, and the book became a mainstay of self-help shelves.

11. E. L. James originally self-published her erotic romance novel *Fifty Shades of Grey*. In 2012, Amazon announced that it had sold more copies of James's book than the whole Harry Potter series combined.

12. Another self-published hit was *The Shack* by Canadian author William P. Young. Released in 2007, its popularity among the Christian community led to word-of-mouth success and sales of over 20 million.

13. Book clubs helped to popularise *The Kite Runner* by Afghan-American author Khaled Hosseini when the paperback came out in 2003. It went on to sell 21 million copies worldwide.

14. *The Shadow of the Wind* by Spanish writer Carlos Ruiz Zafón was a European hit in 2001 and was translated into English in 2004. The international bestseller sold over 15 million copies.

15. Sold as 'the next *Gone Girl*', 2015's *The Girl on the Train* by Paula Hawkins went on to occupy the UK's hardback book chart for 20 weeks, a record at the time.

16. 2002's Man Booker prize-winning novel was *Life of Pi* by Yann Martel. The story charts the survival of an Indian boy stranded on a lifeboat in the Pacific Ocean with a Bengal tiger. Ten years later, it was adapted into a film and won four Oscars, more than any other film in 2013.

17. Another huge seller that year was Alice Sebold's *The Lovely Bones*. The rights to the book were purchased personally by director Peter Jackson, who adapted it in 2009.

18. The power of writing and reading was the central theme of 2005's *The Book Thief*, a historical novel by Markus Zusak set during the Nazi regime.

19. Kathryn Stockett's 2009 bestselling novel, *The Help*, set in 1960s Jackson, Mississippi, USA, was the author's first and took her five years to complete.

20. When John Green's *The Fault in Our Stars* came out in 2011, he signed every copy of the first print run – 150,000 books.

Popular Culture

20 Things Everyone Was Wearing

1. New Spanx shapewear received a big publicity boost in 2000 when Oprah Winfrey endorsed the brand on her show.

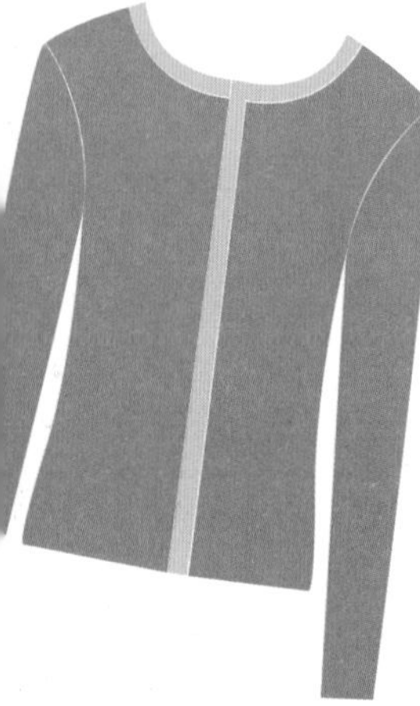

2. When Britney Spears and Justin Timberlake split in 2002, *People* magazine featured a picture of them both wearing Von Dutch trucker caps. A trend was born.

3. Skinny jeans were big business in the 2000s, with the trend really kicking in for women in 2007 and a couple of years later for men.

4. With the rise of skinny jeans came jeggings (denim-style leggings). The word 'jeggings' entered the twelfth edition of the *Concise Oxford English Dictionary* in 2011.

5. Sales of Crocs sandals soared in 2006 – President George W. Bush was photographed wearing them with black socks in 2007.

6. For those not keen on Crocs there was a resurgence of the humble Birkenstock brand in the early 2010s.

7. Juicy Couture tracksuits were the staple uniform of *The Simple Life* star Paris Hilton when the television series first aired in 2003. The brightly coloured velour look was the comfortable way to look cool.

8. To go with your tracksuit, you needed the noughties 'It' bag – a mini, rainbow-coloured Louis Vuitton print handbag, like the kind Lindsay Lohan wore in 2004's film, *Mean Girls.*

9. Before skinnies became the must-have jeans, it was all about low-risers for women – Miss Sixty was the brand *du jour.*

10. Bubble skirts, like the dramatic puff-ball one worn by Carrie Bradshaw in the 2007 *Sex and the City* movie were a popular party look.

11. It was at the Glastonbury Festival in 2004 when actress Sienna Miller was photographed wearing a pair of cosy Ugg boots, and before you knew it, everyone was wearing them.

⓬ In 2003, Nike acquired Converse for around $305 million and continued to market their hugely popular Chuck Taylor All-Stars sneakers.

⓭ Loose-fitting casual jumpsuits started to gain popularity in the late noughties and were being referred to as 'adult onesies' from 2008.

⓮ TOMS shoes officially started selling in 2006. They are famous for their One-for-One business model – where with one purchase of a pair of shoes, the company also gives one pair to a child without shoes. In their first year of business, they sold 10,000 pairs and as a result distributed 10,000 pairs of free shoes to children in Argentina.

⓯ Black ballet flats were a wardrobe staple for most of the 2000s. Ballet flats were initially made popular by Coco Chanel, Audrey Hepburn, Brigitte Bardot and Princess Diana. In the noughties this trendsetting role fell to the likes of Amy Winehouse and British supermodel Kate Moss.

⓰ Invented in 2010 by Malaysian immigrant to the USA, Cheong Choon Ng, the Rainbow Loom is a plastic tool for weaving colourful rubber and plastic bands into decorative bracelets and charms. By 2013, it was one of the most popular toys in the world.

⓱ David Cameron's 2006 unofficially named 'hug a hoodie' speech referred to the popular hoodie sweatshirt that had become a symbol of Britain's disaffected young people.

⓲ The utilitarian belt bag (or fanny pack) emerged as the men's must-have bag of 2017. In 2018, the very roomy 'giant totes' handbags (previously popular in the 2000s) were also making a comeback.

⓳ Bubble shirts or popcorn shirts, as they were also known, were the must-have teen item of 2001. These one-hit wonder crinkly shirts were super small and stretched out to fit.

⓴ French designer Isabel Marant introduced the popular wedged trainers in the early 2010s. The combination high heels hidden in a trainer design soon became a mainstream must-have.

20 Hair and Beauty Trends

1. In 2012, Kim Kardashian posted a before-and-after selfie that gave a revealing insight into how her make-up artist used light and shade to contour her face, a previously mostly industry-only technique. Contouring became the make-up trend of the decade.

2. In the 1990s, thin, heavily plucked eyebrows were the way to go, so by the 2000s, many women were having to fill in their overplucked brows using make-up to create thin, long brows with a high arch.

3. But by the mid-2010s, thick, natural brows were back in style. And with the trend came a new way to achieve the brows of your dreams: microblading, a semi-permanent make-up tattoo like treatment to create fuller-looking eyebrows.

4. Boy band members like Justin Timberlake and Lance Bass were fans of the frosted tips (bleached blond hair spikes) trend of the early 2000s.

5. Another one was self-tanning. In September 2011, the BBC reported that leading self-tanning product company ST.TROPEZ sells three bottles of its bronzing mousse a minute around the world.

6. Tattooing became mainstream in the 2010s. An 18-country study in 2018 showed that 38 per cent of respondents had at least one tattoo, with Italy leading the ranking (48 per cent). Age-wise, more 30- to 49-year-olds than 14- to 29-year-olds have tattoos (45 per cent to 32 per cent). And contrary to popular belief, more women (40 per cent) than men (36 per cent) are inked.

7. Navel piercing reached a peak in 2005 after the stomach-baring pop performances of artists like Christina Aguilera, Janet Jackson, Shakira and Britney Spears had cemented their popularity.

8. The world had fully embraced the man bun by 2015 when online retailer ASOS announced a launch for a new product: a clip-on man bun. It was on April Fool's Day.

9. And men were also encouraged to grow a full beard, a 2010s trend that, at the time of writing, shows no sign of abating. Since 2004 the Movember Foundation has also seen men sporting moustaches to raise money for men's health charities.

10. Glittery make-up (from frosted lip gloss to eye gels and roll-on body sticks) were the make-up statement of the late 1990s and early 2000s.

11. Flesh tunnels and ear plugs became more popular in the late 2000s. By 2011, there were more DIY kits on the market and a wide choice of jewellery.

12. In 2010, the teeth-whitening industry was estimated to be worth $15 billion in the United States alone as people spent big in search of the perfect smile.

13. The Brazilian bikini wax reached a pop-culture pinnacle when it was mentioned on *Sex and the City*. A very hairless trend had taken off.

14. Fake eyelashes became mainstream in the 2000s and started to be sold alongside make-up. In 2004, Madonna wore a pair of mink and diamond lashes worth $10,000.

15. Silky straight hair was a huge trend in the first two decades of the century. In 2016, newspapers reported that 63 per cent of working women in the United Kingdom straightened their hair every day.

16. Lancôme's Juicy Tubes launched in 2000, fuelling the trend for glossy lips and were a make-up bag staple. In 2016 the brand announced their Juicy Shakers in homage to the popular noughties product.

17. Tiger-striped dyed hair, with chunky distinctive highlights, was the way to go if you wanted to make a statement in the late nineties and early noughties.

18. Balayage – a more natural, subtle hair colouring, painted on freestyle, rather than using foils – became the fashion in the 2010s, as soft waves took over from poker straight locks.

19. Cosmetic surgery procedures, such as breast augmentation and face lifts, were fashionable in the 2000s for those who could afford them. In 2010, reality TV star Heidi Montag had ten surgeries in a single day to transform her body and face.

20. Non-surgical cosmetic procedures, such as Botox injections, grew dramatically in popularity in the 2010s. Statistics from the American Society of Plastic Surgeons showed that since 2010 the biggest rise had been in 20- to 29-year-olds.

20 FASHION WEEK HIGHS AND LOWS

1. At London Fashion Week (LFW) in 2000, Hussein Chalayan turned four chair covers and a coffee table into four dresses and a wooden skirt, all in front of the live audience.
2. It was the same year a young Victoria Beckham took to the catwalk for the first time, not yet as a designer but as a model dressed in Maria Grachvogel.
3. It was also when musician and supermodel Grace Jones strutted her stuff on the roof of a limousine at hat designer Philip Treacy's show.
4. In New York that same year, animal rights organisation People for the Ethical Treatment of Animals (PETA) threw red paint on the runway at Randolph Duke's show, hitting his stylist Phillip Bloch.
5. In 2002, Jean Paul Gaultier's Paris show defied gender stereotypes by dressing some of the female models as men. The audience watched the show while listening to erotic novel extracts through headphones.
6. PETA took to New York Fashion Week (NYFW) once again in 2003 during Michael Kors' show. They pelted tofu pies at the front row where *Vogue*'s Anna Wintour and actress Sarah Jessica Parker were sitting.
7. In September 2005, NYFW guests faced more serious injuries at Diane von Furstenberg's spring 2006 show finale, when a bank of hot stage lights crashed down on the front row, injuring a number of high-profile fashion editors and resulting in a few expensive lawsuits.
8. Karl Lagerfeld's stand-out shows include his jaw-dropping $10 million Fendi spectacular held on the Great Wall of China in 2007 and his 'jumbo jet' set for Chanel in 2012.
9. Prince put on a surprise performance in 2008 when he delighted the crowd at Matthew Williamson's spring/summer LFW show.
10. Adidas by Stella McCartney took sportswear to new heights at LFW in 2009 when Olympic gymnast Beth Tweddle and trampolinists took part in the show.
11. Actress Lindsay Lohan took an unsuccessful stab at fashion in 2010 with a brief stint as artistic advisor to Emanuel Ungaro. She introduced heart-shaped glitter pasties to the brand.

⑫ Supermodel Kate Moss lit up the runway in more ways than one when she walked the Louis Vuitton 2011 Paris runway smoking a cigarette. It was on National No Smoking Day.

⑬ In 2012, at Joanna Mastroianni's show in New York, 95-year-old fashion icon Zelda Kaplan collapsed on the front row and was pronounced dead at the hospital later that day.

⑭ *Zoolander* stars Ben Stiller and Owen Wilson brought their model characters, Derek Zoolander and Hansel, to Paris Fashion Week in 2015, gracing the catwalk of Valentino's show.

⑮ Fashion wasn't the only thing on display in Paris that year – at Rick Owen's autumn/winter show the models walked the catwalk with their genitals showing.

⑯ Chanel's 2015 autumn/winter couture collection was staged in a casino set where stars like Kristen Stewart and Julianne Moore played poker while the models walked around them.

⑰ Model Bella Hadid had to deal with every model's worst nightmare when she tumbled over while walking the runway at the 2016 Michael Kors show during NYFW. Turning a corner, she lost her balance in her sky-high heels.

⑱ NYFW's model line-up in 2017 included Jeremy Meeks, a convicted felon whose mugshot went viral in 2014. He received a modelling contract when he was released.

⑲ Kanye West's 2016 Yeezy show made headlines for all the wrong reasons – the show started late, guests had to be bussed to the island location, and the outdoor catwalk in blistering heat saw models fainting.

⑳ In 2018, NYFW ended with the first-ever Savage X Fenty fashion show – a lingerie label from singer-songwriter Rihanna. The elaborate catwalk featured women of different sizes, including pregnant models.

20 THINGS THAT BROKE THE INTERNET

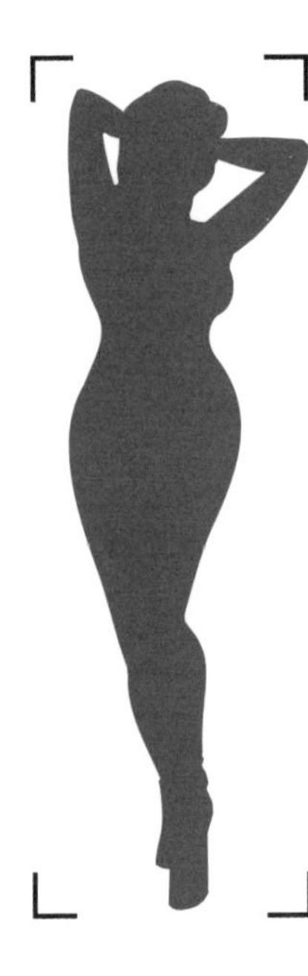

1 When Kim Kardashian posed nude for *Paper* magazine in 2014, the accompanying article was called 'Break the Internet'. And the provocative pictures did just that.

2 In 2017, teenager Carter Wilkerson took the record for most retweets from Ellen DeGeneres' famous Oscar selfie. He cheekily asked American fast food chain Wendy's 'How many retweets for a year of free chicken nuggets?'. Their answer '18 million' started a #NuggsForCarter craze, eventually reaching 3.42 million retweets. Carter still got his nuggets and a $100,000 charity donation in his name.

3 Carter's record was broken in January 2019. Not totally relying on charm, Japanese billionaire Yusaka Maezawa offered online users the chance to win a share of 100 million yen ($1.25 million) if they retweeted his. He succeeded and managed more than 5 million retweets at the time of publication.

4 When a fresco of Christ in a Spanish church needed restoring, 81-year-old Cecilia Giménez gave it her best shot. The truly terrible restoration became a meme and #MonkeyChrist was born.

5 In 2013, supermodel Gisele posted a photo of herself getting glammed up while breastfeeding. The internet went nuts.

6 The Duchess of Cambridge's 2015 photographs of Prince George holding his baby sister Princess Charlotte were widely praised and shared around the world.

7 In 2014, over 6,000 people pledged over $55,000 on Kickstarter to help a man make a potato salad. He ended up throwing a potato-themed party for all his pledgers.

8 At the time of writing, the most liked post on Instagram is a simple photo of a single egg (over 53.2 million likes). It was posted by a mysterious entity called the Egg Gang supposedly representing 'Henrietta', a chicken from the British countryside. The photo was a deliberate attempt to break Kylie Jenner's 2018 record, which showed the first photo of her newborn daughter.

9 When singer Selena Gomez revealed she had had a kidney transplant in 2017, the internet was shocked to say the least.

10 2015 was the year of 'the dress' – a photo of a striped dress that revealed the differences in colour perception, with some saying the dress was black and blue and others saying it was white and gold.

11. Renée Zellweger took a substantial career break in the 2010s. When she was seen on the red carpet in 2014, there was wild internet speculation about the changes in her appearance.

12. In 2013, Beyoncé surprised everyone, including her fans, when she released her fifth studio album with accompanying videos on iTunes without any warning.

13. The summer of 2014 saw the great and the good performing the Ice Bucket Challenge (dumping a bucket of ice-cold water over their heads) to raise money for motor neurone disease.

14. In 2014, tabloid news website TMZ released a video that appeared to show hip-hop star Jay-Z fighting with his sister-in-law Solange in an elevator. It was the shocking footage everyone was watching.

15. One Direction fans were heartbroken when it was announced that Zayn Malik had quit the band. The group's huge online following rallied round, with some organising candlelit vigils.

16. Canadian singer Drake released the video for his single 'Hotline Bling' in 2015. His dance moves inspired countless covers and parodies, including one by his own dad and a commercial from T-Mobile during the 2016 Super Bowl featuring Drake himself.

17. Beyoncé announced she was pregnant with twins in 2017 with a photoshoot of her seated in a bed of flowers holding her bare stomach. It was the most-liked Instagram post that year.

18. 2015 was the year the Charlie Charlie challenge, a modern incarnation of the Spanish paper-and-pencil game, swept the English-speaking internet. The Magic 8-Ball type game was particularly popular with teenagers.

19. Steve Harvey slipped up while announcing the winner of Miss Universe in 2015 – Miss Colombia celebrated her 'win' for more than two minutes before it was announced Miss Philippines was the real winner.

20. The 2014 celebrity phone-hacking scandal saw a number of A-list celebrities, including Jennifer Lawrence, have private information, including naked photos, released online. A number of hackers, later convicted to 8–18 months in prison, joined in on the craze, taking on multiple A-listers in an attempt to expose their private images.

20 Foods that Everyone Was Eating

1. Pastry hybrids like the croissant-doughnut pastry Cronut from Dominique Ansel Bakery in New York meant big business and bigger queues. In 2013 it was named one of the best 'extremely fun' inventions of the year by *Time* magazine.

2. Juicing and smoothies soared in popularity in the 2000s. In the UK alone, the market for packaged crushed-fruit drinks doubled year-on-year between 2001 and 2006.

3. Australian millennials were told their Instagram-worthy avocado breakfasts were the reason they couldn't afford to buy property in a widely distributed newspaper column in 2016.

4. Alternative milks, such as soy, almond, oat and coconut, made themselves a mainstay in the market with a 2018 Mintel report stating that US sales alone have grown 61 per cent since 2012.

5. A 2015 *The New York Times* story about bone broth saw a huge surge in artisanal broth offerings from food outlets on both sides of the Atlantic.

6. Coconut water became the must-have accessory of gym goers and gym posers at the start of the 2010s. Sales of pre-packaged coconut water drinks doubled in 2011 in the United States.

7. Supermarkets in the UK saw a huge boom in sales of Japanese ingredients, particularly miso paste, with Sainsbury's supermarket chain reporting in 2016 of a 32.5 per cent increase in sales in the past twelve months.

8. New Zealand chain Gourmet Burger Kitchen opened its first UK restaurant in 2001. Upmarket burgers have seen a meteoric rise around the world since chains like Byron, Shake Shack and Five Guys have opened in international locations.

9. *Sex and the City* is often credited with popularising the humble cupcake after a 2000 episode saw Carrie and Miranda sitting outside Magnolia Bakery in New York munching on the frosted treats.

10. Coffee consumption in the UK alone soared between 2008 and 2018, from a respectable 70 million cups per day to a caffeine-fuelled 95 million. It is still dwarfed by around 165 million daily cups of tea.

11 The 2010s saw bacon being added to everything, from maple-bacon donuts to bacon-flavoured ice cream, and even 'baconnaise' (a bacon-flavoured mayonnaise that sold 40,000 jars in its first six months in 2008).

12 Quinoa wasn't commonly consumed in North America and Europe until the twenty-first century. As a result, between 2006 and 2013 quinoa crop prices tripled.

13 In 2008, there was one working gin distillery in London. By 2018, there were 24. And the UK Wine and Spirit Trade Association reported that there were at least 100 British gin brands on the market that year.

14 2018 was a year of big business for veganism, especially in the UK, which launched more new plant-based products than any other nation.

15 The start of the 2010s saw gluten-free products become widespread, with a 44 per cent rise in the United States between 2011 and 2013. By 2017, it was a $10.5 billion-dollar industry.

16 The must-have gadget in 2015 was a spiraliser. As a result, ribbons of courgette replaced carb-heavy pasta. Two years later though spiraliser sales had plummeted by 40 per cent.

17 Kombucha tea's popularity has been growing steadily throughout the 2010s. In 2016, Pepsi put their hat in the ring by purchasing KeVita, one of the US's most popular kombucha tea brands.

18 'Freakshakes' are thought to be the invention of a Canberra café owner. The Australian 'delicacy' is an overindulgent milkshake topped with lashings of cream, chocolate and caramel sauces, and delicacies such as chunks of brownie, nuts, pretzels, biscuits and even whole slices of pie. From 2017 on they spread far and wide.

19 A twenty-first-century craft beer craze came out of the brewing trends in the United States and soon small breweries were popping up all over the United Kingdom too.

20 2015's favourite superfood was coconut oil – the fat was being used to cook, eat and even moisturise, with celebrity endorsements aplenty.

20 REALITY TV SHOWS

1. *Big Brother* launched in the UK in 2000. The originally Dutch TV format saw strangers living in a house together followed by cameras. It was franchised to 54 countries and regions.

2. The American series of *Survivor* debuted in 2000 and saw competitors living in an isolated location, providing their own food and shelter and competing in challenges for a $1 million prize.

3. 2001 saw the first series of *The Amazing Race* on American screens. The international travel competition has had versions in Vietnam, Israel and Ukraine, among others.

4. *The Bachelor*, which launched in 2002 on American Television channel ABC, saw beautiful women competing to win the heart of one eligible man. The show has spawned multiple spin-offs including *The Bachelorette*.

5. Airing for the first time in 2002, *The Osbornes* became MTV's most-watched TV series ever. The show was one of the first to give viewers a behind-the-scenes look at celebrity lives and its impact on the TV landscape was significant.

6. The British TV show *Pop Idol*, which only ran for two series, had huge success around the world, particularly in America where *American Idol* is still an annual television event. It launched the careers of Kelly Clarkson, Carrie Underwood, Jennifer Hudson and Adam Lambert.

7. It was shortly followed in 2004 by Simon Cowell's *The X Factor*, which has had 15 seasons so far in the UK and gave the world One Direction, Little Mix and Leona Lewis.

8. Supermodel Tyra Banks helped create *America's Next Top Model*, which started airing in 2003. As of 2018 there have been 24 series of the modelling competition.

9. Fashion was also front and centre when *Project Runway* debuted in 2004 on Netflix. Now in season 17, the competition pits amateur fashion designers against each other in a battle of creativity.

10. 2004 also saw people competing to lose the most weight for a cash prize on *The Biggest Loser.* The American show has been widely criticised and has had spin-offs in over 30 countries.

11. When the BBC revived ballroom dancing in 2004 for its celebrity competition *Strictly Come Dancing*, it would have been surprised to know the show was still a primetime hit after 16 more series and international spin-offs.

12. The E! cable network hit the big time in 2007 when they started filming a fly-on-the-wall look at the lives of the Kardashian family for *Keeping Up With The Kardashians.*

13. *The Hills* started airing on MTV in 2006 – a semi-scripted 'reality' show that followed the lives of a group of friends living and working in Beverly Hills.

14. 'Normal people' became the subject of MTV's 2009 smash hit *Jersey Shore*, which used remote-controlled cameras as well as 12 handheld ones for a documentary feel.

15. Britain's 2010 answer to *The Hills* and *Jersey Shore* was ITV's *The Only Way is Essex* – a structured reality show focusing on the lives of people in Essex where 'some of what they do has been set up purely for your entertainment'.

16. NBC's *The Apprentice* offered business people the chance to compete for a $250,000 contract with Donald Trump as the show's host. The British version started airing in 2005 with Alan Sugar as the prospective employer.

17. Inspired by drama series *Desperate Housewives*, *The Real Housewives* franchise initially chronicled the lives of wealthy women in Orange County, California, USA, in 2006. Since then, different *The Real Housewives* series have been set in over 18 other locations.

18. MTV's 2009 series *16 and Pregnant* and its spin-off *Teen Mom* gave an unfiltered look at life as a teenage parent, in an effort to promote the practice of safe sex.

19. While it only lasted four years in the UK, Gordon Ramsay's *Hell's Kitchen* continues to be a success in the United States, where two teams of chefs compete for a job in a top kitchen.

20. Watching scantily clad men and women cavort on *Love Island* was something viewers in the UK couldn't resist. Almost three million viewers watched the opening episode in 2018.

20 Fads for Getting Fit

1. Toning shoes like MBTs, launched in 2000, and FitFlops, in 2007, promised to transform your legs and buttocks while you walked. By 2012 toning shoe sales in the United States had become a $1 billion industry.

2. High-intensity interval training (HIIT), with short bursts of intense activity, based on sports science research like Izumi Tabata's 1996 study became the way to work out.

3. Dance aerobic workout Zumba was founded in 2001 in Miami, Florida, USA. By 2013 it had 14 million weekly participants in 150 countries.

4. Throughout the 2010s, yoga became more and more mainstream in the West. In America the number of people doing yoga grew by 50 per cent between 2012 and 2016.

5. With a growth in yoga's popularisation came new forms of the practice: baby yoga, dog yoga and yoga with goats, to name a few.

6. Fitness became digital with the introduction of apps and wearable technologies. Fitbit launched their first Fitbit Flex in 2013. The wristband measures and analyses fitness-related data such as the number of steps walked, calories burned, heart rate, sleep quality or steps climbed.

7. North American sales for Kangoo Jumps, Swiss-engineered boots with plastic springs, quadrupled in 2008 as group exercise classes became popular.

8. The rising popularity of running led to the establishment of Parkrun, a regular group running event in London. The Parkrun idea soon spread around the world. In 2018, there were five million registered runners.

9. Amateur marathon running also saw a huge spike in popularity, and so did new 'fun runs' like The Color Run, held in over 50 North American cities in 2012, and Tough Mudder, an endurance event series started in 2010 in the United States, in which participants work

together on obstacle courses about 16–19 kilometres (10–12 miles) in length, which test mental and physical strength.

10. In 2009, a Shake Weight dumbbell infomercial went viral. It featured a version of the traditional exercising weight modified to shake vigorously and was even parodied on *Saturday Night Live*.

11. The fitness regime CrossFit was developed in 2000 by Greg Glassman and Lauren Jenai. The brand's original gym was in Santa Cruz, California, USA. By 2016 there were 13,000 affiliated gyms around the world.

12. Spinning had been popular since the 1990s, but indoor cycling classes at SoulCycle took over New York, USA, and beyond in the late 2000s, transforming the workout.

13. Kettlebell training was the exercise *du jour* in the mid 2000s when workout DVDs promised a full-body transformation using the weight. Celebrities like Geri Halliwell swore by it.

14. Pole fitness classes started to pop up from 2003 in gyms and dance studios. The first Pole World Cup was held in 2005 in Amsterdam, the Netherlands. The 2018 championship in Fort Lauderdale, Florida, USA featured competitors from 38 countries.

15. Barefoot running and minimalist running shoes saw a huge rise in popularity after the 2009 publication of Christopher McDougall's *Born to Run*.

16. In 1999, the British government introduced a cycle-to-work scheme that allows people to offset the costs tax-free. It coincided with a twenty-first-century bike boom, with sales of road bikes and cycling gear on the rise year-on-year.

17. Exergaming, where physical activity is combined with video games, was also on the rise. Wii Fit was released in 2007 and saw Nintendo Wii users take on yoga, strength training, balance and aerobic activities from the comfort of their homes.

18. More traditional dance workouts, including salsa, hip-hop and ballet barre fitness, became a staple offering in the 2000s.

19. From yoga retreats to cycling tours, the adventure and activity holiday sector saw a rise of 65 per cent between 2011 and 2015.

20. Both Britney Spears' 2008 album *Circus* and Pink's aerial dances at her concerts inspired a new wave of young people to try circus classes.

20 Hashtags

1 #BlackLivesMatter is the hashtag of the international activist movement against violence and racism towards black people. The hashtag was originated in 2013 after the acquittal of neighbourhood watchman George Zimmerman for the shooting of African-American teenager Trayvon Martin.

2 In 2017, #MeToo went viral after sex abuse allegations against Hollywood producer Harvey Weinstein started a global movement against sexual harassment and assault.

3 #TakeAKnee started trending in the wake of the August 2016 protest by NFL players who refused to stand up during the National Anthem and instead sat down or knelt – a silent protest against social injustice and oppression.

4 In May 2017, Donald Trump addressed the media in a tweet starting with 'Despite the constant negative press covfefe'. The misspelling of coverage and the denial by Trump's spokesman Sean Spicer meant that #Covfefe soon went viral, becoming a widespread joke.

5 Trump triggered the #DressLikeAWoman hashtag in 2017 when he reportedly told his female staff to do so. Women accompanied the retweeting of the hashtag with photos of what they wear to work.

6 The #StopFundingHate campaign was started in 2016 by UK writer Richard Wilson. It called on companies, such as Asda, British Airways and LEGO to stop advertising in *The Sun*, the *Daily Mail* and the *Daily Express* newspapers.

7 The United Nation's #HeForShe is a solidarity campaign that encourages all genders to work towards gender equality. Its launch was hosted by UN Women Goodwill Ambassador and actress Emma Watson.

8 A video of the aftermath of a knife attack at London's Leytonstone underground station in 2015 showed the attacker pinned to the floor and a bystander shouting: 'You ain't no Muslim, bruv.' The phrase soon formed a hashtag #YouAintNoMuslimBruv that trended on Twitter.

9 January 2017 was the month that #WomensMarch made the news – women and men around the world marched for equal rights in the wake of Donald Trump's inauguration.

10 Even First Lady Michelle Obama and the Pope took to Twitter with #BringBackOurGirls to demand the return of 276 female students who were kidnapped by Boko Haram in Chibok, Nigeria.

11 #JeSuisCharlie and #PrayForParis were some of the most popular hashtags in 2015, the year that multiple terrorist attacks took place in the French capital.

12 A grassroots protest movement that began in 2016 in response to the approved construction of the Dakota Access Pipeline through the Standing Rock Indian Reservation was soon known by #NODAPL.

13 Social media reacted with the hashtag #IStandWithAhmed when 14-year-old American science enthusiast Ahmed Mohammed was arrested. In September 2015, a homemade clock he brought into school was mistaken by one teacher for a bomb. Five policemen came to arrest him.

14 #YesAllWomen has been used widely since 2014 to share stories about violence against women and misogyny in response to #NotAllMen and following the Isla Vista killings in California, USA, in 2014.

15 #Ferguson trended in March 2015 during the unrest in the American city in response to the fatal shooting of African-American Michael Brown by a police officer the previous year.

16 Actress Jameela Jamil started the #IWeigh hashtag in 2018 in response to the focus on women's body weights. She encouraged others to share what they 'weigh' 'beyond their flesh and bones'.

17 When in 2015 the Supreme Court ruled in favour of same-sex marriage in the United States, legalising it in all 50 states, #LoveWins was the hashtag that people used to celebrate.

18 As revolution spread across the Middle East in late 2010 and beyond, #ArabSpring was trending hugely in the region and around the world.

19 #DogsAtPollingStations first appeared on Twitter in 2017 when the Dogs Trust in the UK encouraged voters to bring their pooches to the ballot box with them.

20 After the riots in London in 2011, people took to social media to organise a clean-up. #RiotCleanUp was the hashtag that helped people show their solidarity.

IMAGE CREDITS

p.4 – eagle © Aleksandr Sulga/Shutterstock.com; warning sign © Maksim M/ Shutterstock.com; athletes © Aleksandr Sulga/Shutterstock.com; map point © D Line/Shutterstock.com; cupcake © Arizzona Design/Shutterstock.com; dog © NadzeyaShanchuk/Shutterstock.com; motorbike © kstudija/Shutterstock.com; thumbs up © sundora14/Shutterstock.com; musical note © Sylfida/Shutterstock.com; money © rzarek/Shutterstock.com; comb © Olli_may/Shutterstock.com; clothing © Fotinia/ Shutterstock.com; remote © hvostik/Shutterstock.com; airplane © B. Melo/Shutterstock. com; palm tree © Pogorelova Olga/Shutterstock.com; emoji © flower travelin' man/ Shutterstock.com; singer © Paper Wings/Shutterstock.com; game controller © Alexandr III/Shutterstock.com; rings © Nobelus/Shutterstock.com; computer © krzysmam/Shutterstock.com; trophy holder © Edvard Molnar/Shutterstock.com; planet © Macrovector/Shutterstock.com; skull © Lemberg Vector studio/Shutterstock. com; butterfly © Tshooter/Shutterstock.com; helicopter © vadimmmus/Shutterstock. com; orange © Inspiring/Shutterstock.com; phone © Aleksangel/Shutterstock.com; Segway © dovla982/Shutterstock.com; pp.6/7 © amgun/Shutterstock.com; pp.8/9 – cogs © superbank stock/Shutterstock.com; crane © Pand P Studio/Shutterstock. com; pp.10/11 © Binly/Shutterstock.com; pp.12/13 © khis dryawan/Shutterstock.com; pp.14/15 – controller © Alexandr III/Shutterstock.com; handheld console © Martial Red/Shutterstock.com; pp.16/17 – mobile devices © Aleksangel/Shutterstock.com; emojis © flower travelin' man/Shutterstock.com; selfie poser © Natalia Toropova/ Shutterstock.com; pp.20/21 – motorbike © kstudija/Shutterstock.com; racing car © Robcartorres/Shutterstock.com; tarmac © Machalski/Shutterstock.com; pp.22/23 – segway rider © dovla982/Shutterstock.com; hoverboard rider © Pavel K/Shutterstock. com; pp.24/25 © Bruno Ismael Silva Alves/Shutterstock.com; pp.26/27 – skyline © bioraven/Shutterstock.com; airplane © B. Melo/Shutterstock.com; pp.28/29 © D Line/Shutterstock.com; pp.30/31 – globe © peiyang/Shutterstock.com; boat © oxameel/Shutterstock.com; airplane © B. Melo/Shutterstock.com; pp.32/33 © WladD/ Shutterstock.com; pp.34/35 – galaxy © ASAG Studio/Shutterstock.com; planets © Macrovector/Shutterstock.com; pp.36/37 – pots © Odrinna/Shutterstock.com; bones © Lemberg Vector studio/Shutterstock.com; pp.38/39 © solar22/Shutterstock.com; pp.40/41 – hexagon pattern © matthew25/Shutterstock.com; doctor/patient © one line man/Shutterstock.com; pp.42/43 – eagle © Aleksandr Sulga/Shutterstock.com; monkey © nikiteev_konstantin; chameleon © Kozyreva Elena/Shutterstock.com; fish © Tshooter/ Shutterstock.com; pp.44/45 © MIKHAIL GRACHIKOV/Shutterstock.com; pp.46/47 © Maxim Kulikov/Shutterstock.com; pp.48/49 – texture © Simon Tang/Shutterstock. com; dinosaurs © DianaFinc/Shutterstock.com; pp.50/51 © MarijaPiliponyte/